SHOT DOWN

SHOT DOWN

A SECRET DIARY OF ONE POW'S LONG MARCH TO FREEDOM

ALEX KERR

Pen & Sword
AVIATION

First published in 2015 by Big Sky Publishing Ltd
PO Box 303, Newport, NSW 2106, Australia

Republished in this format in 2016 by
Pen & Sword AVIATION
An imprint of
Pen & Sword Books Ltd
47 Church Street, Barnsley
South Yorkshire
S70 2AS

Copyright © Alex Kerr 2015, 2016

ISBN 978 1 47387 802 0

Typeset by Think Productions

Printed and bound in England
By CPI Group (UK) Ltd, Croydon, CR0 4YY

Pen & Sword Books Ltd incorporates the Imprints of Pen & Sword Aviation,
Pen & Sword Family History, Pen & Sword Maritime, Pen & Sword Military,
Pen & Sword Discovery, Pen & Sword Politics, Pen & Sword Atlas,
Pen & Sword Archaeology, Wharncliffe Local History, Leo Cooper,
Wharncliffe True Crime, Wharncliffe Transport, Pen & Sword Select,
Pen & Sword Military Classics, The Praetorian Press, Claymore Press,
Remember When, Seaforth Publishing and Frontline Publishing

For a complete list of Pen & Sword titles please contact
PEN & SWORD BOOKS LIMITED
47 Church Street, Barnsley, South Yorkshire, S70 2AS, England
E-mail: enquiries@pen-and-sword.co.uk
Website: www.pen-and-sword.co.uk

To my wife
Joan Ivy Kerr
1921–2000

CONTENTS

SHOT DOWN

FOREWORD

It was a great honour to be asked to write a foreword to this story because it is a story that resonates greatly with me, as it is very similar to my father's story. Like Alex Kerr, my father was also shot down as a very young man, incarcerated for the remainder of his war in Stalag Luft III and at the very end of the war marched across Northern Europe in bitter winter conditions, emerging from the whole experience a man of great resilience and integrity.

This book is a fascinating read and at the same time a careful and accurate record of life in the POW camps. Alex Kerr states in his epilogue that he set out to give an account of his days as a POW in the Second World War based on his diaries, which he kept meticulously during his incarceration. These diaries were transcribed directly and the background narrative added later, with a view to providing a historical, factual account of that period of our war history. Throughout *Shot Down* the author gives a very matter-of-fact account of his whole experience of being shot down, wounded and imprisoned at the age of 20. There are no complaints or emotional self-indulgence, and yet the author paints a very clear picture of life in the camp. His strength, courage and devotion to his mates, his supreme optimism and determination to make the best of any situation, come through the narrative on every page. Occasionally however, we get glimpses of the pain, despair and futility that he must have felt at times. He manages to encapsulate the whole POW experience in his description of the gift of an egg, an unheard-of luxury, on his 21st birthday, from a fellow prisoner he hardly knew. The hunger that was almost always with them is suddenly brought into clear focus. He dismisses his own efforts to escape lightly and gives a fascinating account of his escape from the Death March, his journey to the Allied lines and his final self-repatriation back to England.

Air Chief Marshal Sir Angus Houston AK, AFC (Ret'd)

PROLOGUE

The German ambulance bumped and swayed as it sped in the dark along the rough country road. Its headlights, striving to shine through the meagre wartime slits, broke the darkness and lit up the road ahead with a narrow beam.

The rough movement of the ambulance threw me from one side of the stretcher to the other, making me strain against the leather straps which held me in. My breathing was laboured. I was in pain, but it was more mental than physical. I was bleeding from my chest, my arm and my leg in a sticky mixture of torn leather, torn fur, and torn flesh and blood. It was not a pleasant sight.

As I fought for each breath and recalled what had happened to me I became convinced more than ever that I did not have much more than minutes to live. So several times I tried unsuccessfully to end the pain quickly by holding my breath. The effort exhausted me and I lay back to await the end with resignation. I drifted off to sleep thinking back on my life and to where it all started.

CHAPTER 1
ANTIQUITY

My father, Bill Kerr, was born in Scotland in 1880 and, after service in South Africa in the Boer War, immigrated to Australia. Here he met Lillian Weight, who had been born in New South Wales in the same year, but was by then living in Victoria with other members of her family. They were married in Toorak in 1903. They lost their first baby — a boy — and then in 1906 had another boy, William Langford.

After Bill had been plying up and down the eastern seaboard as a ship's engineer, the couple set out by ship for Western Australia with the baby. My brother was christened William Langford but known throughout his life as Langford, presumably to avoid confusion with my father, who was also William. The ship's voyage ended at Albany so they disembarked there and made their way by land to Perth. Bill's first job was with a large hardware firm — Harris Scarfe and Sandovers — which handled machinery and other equipment. He was a trained engineer and Scottish engineers were in demand in those days.

The first of many moves in their new state came when Bill was given the task of installing a suction gas engine and setting up a power station to give electric light to Southern Cross, a town which was fast becoming an important communication and population centre on the line from Perth to Kalgoorlie. It was there that Freda was born, in 1909, and Frances the following year. About 1912 a similar assignment saw the family move to Kellerberrin where Bill's task was to install the town's power plant and then spend a year or so training an operator to run the plant.

This completed, the family moved back to Perth and took up residence in West Leederville. After a brief stay there Bill was on the road again, this time to Albany to install the power plant there. After completion the family moved back to West Leederville once more. Thus ended a period during which Bill was in demand for installing power plants in the young growing towns in fledgling Western Australia, substituting electric light for candle light and oil lamps.

It was at the time of the outbreak of World War I in Europe that Bill joined the staff of Hoskens Foundry in Perth to run its power plant. Along with several other companies it was owned by mining entrepreneur Claude De Bernales. De Bernales was a very wealthy man. A rogue is how many would have described him, much of his money having been made through dubious mining ventures. He used some of his money to construct a large mansion at Cottesloe. Bill was responsible for supervising the electrical installations. The mansion later became the Cottesloe Civic Centre.

Bill recalled the early days in the outback when he would wait on his motorcycle outside some mining tenement, ready to start the motor for a quick getaway. More than once a fleet-footed De Bernales, pursued by an irate miner who felt he had been fleeced, would sprint to the bike, leap on the pillion and the two of them would disappear in a cloud of red dust. It was his mining ventures, promoted so successfully in London, and his dubious business ethics — to give them the most charitable interpretation — which eventually brought about his downfall and subjected him to the humiliation of a public trial at the Old Bailey. By this time Bill had long left his service and moved into the oil business.

He recalled other incidents in the then colourful Western Australian outback where, even though the heady days of the Kalgoorlie and Coolgardie gold rushes had receded into the past, the lure of gold still drew hopefuls from all parts of the globe. His earliest visits there were as a greenhorn Scot, not knowing quite what to expect and having heard hair-raising tales of violence on the 'fields', for self-protection he carried a pistol and slept with it under his pillow.

In a typically grossly overcrowded hotel in Wiluna the dining room was converted after the evening meal into sleeping quarters, with camp stretchers. One night some of the miners decided to have a joke at the expense of the new chum with the Scottish accent. They tied a rope to the leg of his camp stretcher and when he retired early

— as was his wont — they crept in and gave the rope a hearty tug thus dumping a sleeping Bill on the floor. They had not bargained with an armed and very scared Scot who thought murder and mayhem were about to take place. He grabbed his pistol, fired a warning shot into the ceiling and threatened to shoot anyone who came in his sights. It was some time before they could summon the local police constable. He was able to persuade Bill that it was all a practical joke and the much-inconvenienced and chastened hotel patrons were able to get to bed.

In 1917 Bill left Hoskens Foundry and began a new job that was to last for 16 years. He joined the Texas Oil Company as a salesman. Motor cars were increasing rapidly in number and prospects in the oil business appeared bright. But the industry was still in its infancy and selling to the limited market was not easy. At that time the one and only city taxi rank ran along the centre of St George's Terrace and the cabbies were Bill's main source of custom. It was not long before Bill was appointed manager. He enjoyed his new status in the community. In those days the life insurance office managers, the stock company managers, the bank managers and the oil company managers formed a small but influential clique in Perth's business life.

My father was a well-dressed, portly gentleman, genial and friendly, with a pronounced Scotch accent. He had a sense of humour and liked to entertain. I remember him singing Scottish songs and playing records by Harry Lauder, the famous Scottish comedian, on his HMV wind-up gramophone. His greatest hobby was tinkering with cars.

On weekends he donned overalls and immersed himself in car reconstruction and maintenance. He owned a succession of cars in the 1920s and 1930s and claimed that at one time he held the unofficial speed record between Perth and Albany. In his stable of cars, stretching over a period of years, were a 1912 De Dion Bouton, a 1914 Woolsley with gas lamps and a Bianchi body, a 1916 Flanders bought from a Chinese gardener for 10 pounds (Bill completely rebuilt the body), a 1920 Hupmobile, a 1923 Grasshopper Chevrolet, a 1926 Essex six, a 1930 Buick straight eight, a General Motors Marchette and finally a Vauxhall commercial coupe.

He and my brother Langford, who had become a fully qualified marine steam and diesel engineer, always had some kind of project going in the garage, with engine blocks, pistons, conrods, and other bits and pieces of cannibalised cars lying about in cutaway kerosene tins, and chain blocks and tackle suspended from the roofing rafters.

My mother, in contrast to my father, was a tall, quiet, good-looking housewife who always dressed in the fashion of the day and had a dignified demeanour. She always managed to look to be in command of the situation and seemed to me to be the real boss of the Kerr household.

CHAPTER 2
CHILDHOOD, 1921–1929

It was in April 1921 that I came onto the scene. As was common in those days, I was born at home — 109 Northwood Street, West Leederville — with Dr Fred Carter and Nurse Mary Cox in attendance.

Looking back on the 1920s from my perspective as a young child in a middle-class family, and coupling that with what I have learnt subsequently about that era, I am sure that it must have been a great time to have been a young adult. World War I — the 'war to end all wars' — was now comfortably in the past, and Australia was developing rapidly with no hint of the economic pain that was to come from the worldwide Great Depression.

Popular music was jaunty, simple and happy and everyone was dancing to it (the Charleston days); jobs were easy to come by; a new mode of entertainment, the movie, was emerging; that new mode of transport, the motor car, was developing rapidly; and an even newer and more exciting mode, the aeroplane, had arrived on the scene. There would seem to have been no cloud of any sort on the horizon. I think the 'Roaring Twenties' must have epitomised the phrase 'the good old days' to many as they grew older.

I was too young to experience much of that decade, unfortunately, but I certainly have vivid recollections of its declining years from about 1927, when I was six years of age, onward.

Of my early years, one to five, I have very few recollections. One memory that does stand out is of a magnificent three-wheeler bicycle which I am sure must have cost a great deal of money. It was mine and a very beautiful piece of machinery it was; much larger and more substantial than those one sees today. I was very proud of it and treated it well. Apropos that, I have always considered myself lucky to have had a father and a brother who taught me to understand, respect and look after machinery with tender loving care.

Another memory of those early years was a trip that I took with my mother across the Nullarbor by train. I was fascinated by the Aborigines who seemed so black to me. I had a new experience of sleeping in a moving train and was astounded by the miles and miles of endless arid and uninteresting (to me) red plains. There was also the new experience of having to go down to the dining car one evening, minus my mother who was indisposed, to order my meal. At six years of age, I was not up to coping with a menu that was mostly in French and Italian so I drew upon my limited memory of culinary delights and, after looking knowledgeably at the menu, solemnly ordered the only thing I could think of — a leg of lamb!

I commenced school at West Leederville Primary in 1927. This was also the year in which brother Langford decided to try his hand at gold mining. Langford was a strapping 21-year-old, a well-trained mechanic who was later to become Chief Superintending Engineer of the Western Australian State Ships. In the large backyard we had at Northwood Street, he and my father erected the framework of what was to be his home for the next few years. All joists were bolted; it was a very professional job. I have a very clear recollection of that frame standing there. It was then disassembled, transported to the mine site and reassembled. It served as Langford's home for three years.

During those years he and five others worked their mine at Lake Austin in the Murchison — north of Mt Magnet and 14 miles from Cue. They worked the mine to 220 feet but eventually ran out of gold. It had, 30 years before, yielded quite a lot but was now played out. Langford often commuted to Perth on his 2.75 hp AJS motorbike with Prince, his black cloud Kelpie, riding on the petrol tank in front of him. He usually brought down a kangaroo tail for soup and very much appreciated it was too.

One occasion I will never forget occurred in my third year at school. The day was very hot and I was walking up Northwood Street on my way back to school after lunch. I walked in the centre of the road and came across a metal horseshoe which I immediately picked up. It was believed to be a powerful good luck symbol. Remembering that the way to maximise your luck was to spit on the horseshoe and throw it over your left shoulder, I did so immediately and started off to school wondering what good luck would come my way. It was probably only a few seconds before I felt a heavy blow on my head and the horseshoe fell to the ground. So much for good luck! So I continued on my way to school and it was not until sometime later that Miss Green gasped with fright as she saw blood running down both sides of my face. I was sent to the doctor without delay. The memory is still very clear.

Food in the 1920s and 1930s differed in a great many respects from what is generally eaten nowadays. It was less refined and undoubtedly more wholesome. Heart disease was not a topic of conversation, lung cancer was relatively unknown, cholesterol was not on everyone's lips, polyunsaturated fats had never been heard of and any kind of alternative medicines and diets were regarded with the utmost suspicion.

The European influences in food, introduced to the country by the waves of post-war migrants, and the later introduction of the spicier oriental foods, brought in by the groups of Asian refugees from countries torn apart by civil war, had not yet occurred and as a consequence the typical Australian diet was the traditional bland English fare — mostly roasts, stews, bakes and puddings. Even the Aussie 'barbie' had not yet arrived!

Despite the fact that we were reasonably well off, on the whole our meals were simple and cheap compared with what a middle-class family would expect now. Beef, pork, lamb, rabbit, beef sausages and tripe were the staple meats with plenty of cooked vegetables in the winter and plenty of salads in the summer. Bread and dripping was a favourite. Water was drunk with meals. Wine was rare in our house. Chickens, turkeys and all other kinds of birds were delicacies to be savoured only on special occasions. We kept chooks and ducks and it was always my father's job to decapitate the bird when a special occasion was looming, and it was my mother's job to pluck it. The smell of the warm bird being plucked always offended my nose.

In my early recollections of those halcyon days are things which do not exist anymore but which then were accepted, indeed essential, parts of life. The Western Ice cart came regularly in the summer, and from it was dispensed the glistening, dripping blocks of ice for the top of our ice chests. Drawn by a pair of heavy draught horses, cold water dripping from it continuously, it left its transitory trail on the steaming bitumen of the road. John the Chinaman would toil with his horse and cart up Northwood Street, laden with beautifully just-picked vegetables from the market gardens which were at the foot of Northwood Street, a mere eight hundred yards away. The aroma of the fresh produce was so seductive. The bread cart would appear, pulled by one horse, oozing out the heavenly, mouth-watering smell of freshly baked bread. The bake house was in Northwood Street, two hundred yards up the hill from our home. The money for the milkman was always left out in an enamel billy at the front gate where the milkman would ladle out the designated amount. The creamy milk was always delivered in the cool of the night for obvious reasons.

Coolgardie safes were part of every household. With hessian sides moistened by thin strips of linen siphoning water from the tray at the top to reticulate slowly down the sides and hopefully catch air movement, they induced cooling by evaporation. They provided cheap but somewhat ineffectual competition to the ice chests. With no home refrigeration in those days the ice chests themselves, carrying a block of ice in the top compartment, were essential for the short-term preservation of perishable foodstuffs.

Rotary clothes lines were unknown. Clothes were hung on long galvanised wire lines which had to be propped up in the centre to prevent the clothes from dragging on the ground. Aborigines would walk the streets regularly with their cry of 'Props, Props' selling long hand-hewn wooden props. Their black faces and hands used to scare me, as did also those of the Indian and Malay seamen on the ships that we visited occasionally in Fremantle when my father had friends or business acquaintances to visit in port.

Meanwhile my two sisters were working as stenographers in Perth. I used to look forward to Fridays as that was pay day, when my two big sisters would bring me home lollies and other goodies.

In 1928, aunts Mary and Catherine visited briefly from Scotland and in 1931 Freda followed them back to Scotland for a year or so. In the same year Langford quit the mine and came back to Perth where he joined the Texas Oil Company and spent the next two years installing manually operated petrol pumps at the metropolitan garages which were springing up in all suburbs as motor vehicles became the popular means of personal transport. Perth's population was around the quarter-million mark and the main forms of mass transit were the steam train and the electric tram.

The years at West Leederville Primary School were pleasant ones. I lived in the same street as the school and not very far from it so it was no hassle to walk to and from school each day, even when it was raining. I was a reasonably good scholar and thus did not incur the wrath of teachers very often, though I can still feel the pain of the cane hitting my outstretched hands on a cold winter's morning when the headmaster gave me the 'cuts' for some misdemeanour. On the other hand, it was the cold winter mornings that used to herald the 4-gallon kerosene cans full of steaming hot milk from which our enamel mugs were filled.

Once a year the trainee dentists came to set up their dental chairs in the school cloakroom and go about their business of achieving experience and skill by operating on terrified primary school children with a pedal drill and seemingly ineffectual anaesthetics. The cries of pain, anguish and terror were unnerving to those who were trying to concentrate on their lessons in the adjoining classrooms.

Play in those days was really very simple. There was always sport — football in the winter, which required no equipment other than the ball, and cricket in the summer, which required a kerosene case for the wicket, a tennis ball and a piece of wood for the bat. Other sporting and playtime activities included making use of the Northwood Street hill for trolley races. We made our own trolleys very simply — a plank about 12 inches wide and 48 inches long provided the body, with a fixed crosspiece at the rear to take the rear axle and a swiveled crosspiece at the front to take the front axle and to provide steering by rope. Sometimes we even went to the luxury of attaching a brake. Even though cars were scarce in those days we nevertheless always had to station a lookout at the bottom of the long hill to avoid accidents.

Mongers Lake was also a focal point for leisure activities. At the height of the summer we used to swim in the lake after school — half a mile each day — to the Wembley end and back to the jetty and boatshed at Blencowe Street. At the turn of the century boating regattas were held on Mongers Lake. We found that hard to believe as it was not very attractive when we knew it. But it did boast a substantial jetty we used to dive from and a boatshed where the Sea Scouts kept their steel canoes. I and most of my friends belonged to the 135th West Leederville Scout Group.

The Mongers Lake Yacht Club was an exclusive group of boys who all owned their canoes. To qualify for membership one had to have made one's own canoe. Essential materials for this were: a sheet of galvanised roofing iron, preferably without nail holes; some tar or pitch; some nails; and two pieces of wood, one for the transom at the back, and one for the stem at the front. We made our own paddles and sometimes went as far as to fit out the canoes with masts and sails, though without a centreboard they were very unstable in a strong breeze. Rudders were considered too sophisticated and in any case were too hard to build. Some Saturdays we would sail over to the other side of the lake (the north-west corner) with a sack of provisions and on the dried reeds would cook ourselves sausages and onions for lunch, imagining that we were explorers, breaking new territory in some vast unexplored land. The perennial leeches were a nuisance and we always carried matches as we found that burning them off our skin was a quicker and much more effective way of ridding ourselves of the slimy black creatures than trying to pull them off.

The Saturday afternoon movies were also very popular, particularly in the winter when outdoor activities had sometimes to be curtailed. The moving film was a new and exciting entertainment medium and was just making the transition from silent films to sound. Colour was still a thing of the future. The local venue was the Empire Theatre in Cambridge Street. To the viewer nowadays those early films were almost unbelievably 'corny' but to us they were very real. To the accompaniment of shouts and the stamping of many feet, and the playing of the 'William Tell' overture, our cowboy screen heroes, Tom Mix and Hoot Gibson, firing from the hip at full gallop and assisted by subtitles, would chase the baddies into the wide blue yonder where the heroine was usually tied to a tree, waiting to be rescued. We would, while savouring the excitement of the chase, be consuming quantities of broken biscuits bought for three pence from the tuckshop beside the school.

Mondays were always washing days and they would begin early with my mother stoking up the wood-fired copper. The pine copper stick, used to stir the clothes, was worn smooth and bleached almost white and on hot summer days wielding it to turn over the sheets and other large items must have been enervating to say the least. Housewives in that era, without all the labour-saving devices that are taken for granted these days, had to be fit and strong. Of course, everything is relative and their progenitors were expected to do even more than they did. For some time we had a succession of maids but none of them was very satisfactory.

Another regular and, to my mind, most reprehensible and vile custom was for my mother to administer, every Saturday morning, a teaspoon of castor oil, just to ensure regularity.

Music in the house came in various ways. I used to love playing the pianola, or player piano, as we used to call it. We had a goodly collection of 'rolls' with selections from grand opera and Gilbert and Sullivan mixed in with some of the more popular light songs of the time. As well as the pianola we had a His Majesty's Voice portable gramophone and a good selection of 78 rpm records which had a playing time of three minutes. One had to wind the spring each time and select a steel needle from the little container which swivelled out from the corner of the machine. It was just a toy compared with the sophisticated sound systems of today but it gave a lot of pleasure, particularly on picnics and outings. Into the bargain we had the beginnings of radio with the first crystal sets. With two electrical engineers in the house we did not want for these modern day marvels and we used to get the early programs through our rudimentary headphones, including those first test cricket broadcasts by Alan McGilvray in the early 1930s.

I was starting to learn piano at that time from a friend of the family, but I did not make very good progress. I regretted later, of course, that I had not persevered with it. Langford, on the other hand, did learn to play several instruments and set up a dance band with some friends. I well remember one Saturday night, as a small kid, sitting behind the band listening to my brother dispensing music to a group of perspiring dancers somewhere in a hall in Leederville.

It was no doubt the music that I was surrounded with in my childhood that instilled in me a lasting love of and need for music. Just before the war I used to occasionally sing with the Ron Jenkins Band at the Palais de Danse on the Cottesloe beach front and several years later I sang with Ron Bush's 20-piece dance band in a German prison camp as a member of a vocal trio. At the same time, before the war, I was expressing myself musically in another way through the founding and development of a mouth organ band which eventually reached a respectable level of competence.

One very vivid memory of a custom that is no longer extant — at least in Perth — is of our Guy Fawkes or 'bonfire' nights. Preparation would begin well before 5 November, the date on which Guy Fawkes (a fanatical Roman Catholic, who had served in the Spanish Army and had returned to England to mastermind a plot to set fire to and blow up the Houses of Parliament) was apprehended and subsequently beheaded. We would spend days gathering wood and other flammable materials and pile them up on some vacant land nearby ready for 'the bonfire'. Occasionally we would make up a 'Guy' from old cast-off clothes stuffed with straw and any other available material and then parade it down the street and solicit money from the public. As the big day approached we would take our guy down to the West Leederville railway station and set him up at the bottom of the ramp used by the commuters going home from work. There we would rattle our empty jam tins and cry, 'Remember, remember the fifth of November. Remember, remember the fifth of November. Penny for the guy. Penny for the guy.' We used the money we had collected to buy fireworks — catherine wheels, penny bombs, sky rockets, jumping jacks, sparklers, flower pots and tom thumbs which we let off after dark on the night, standing around the blazing bonfire.

My mother was very athletic. She was a great sport lover and good at sport. She was a member of the Leederville Tennis Club for many years and sometimes would take me there on a Saturday afternoon when I was very small. My fondest recollections are of the afternoon teas, particularly the scones with jam and cream! She was also a very good golfer and won several trophies at the Nedlands Golf Club where she was a member. She continued playing until she was 75. Bridge was also a favourite pastime of hers and she was a member of the Perth Bridge Club. My mother had her own car and used it to run me to all the meetings I needed to attend as I joined more and more youth groups. Before I got my driver's licence she used to drive me to the Sunday baseball games which I played in as a member of the Wests Baseball Club. On one occasion, in 1933, she took me to see the great Don Bradman play at the WACA ground. We were in a perfect position to see another century crafted by the master. He made six runs!

My father's ownership of a weekend shack at Mount Pleasant just past the Canning Bridge in the 1920s and early 1930s gave us a holiday home. In those days Mount Pleasant — now so pleasantly developed — was still bush land. The entire area along the river front — The Esplanade, where so many expensive homes are now established — was a dairy farm. We would cross the Canning Bridge and drive alongside the farm on a dirt road until we came to the rise of Mount Pleasant. We would then deflate the tyres and drive the remaining 200 yards of sand track leading to our wood and asbestos shack which came complete with goannas, snakes, scorpions, centipedes and large hairy black huntsman spiders. Just down the hill, at the river's edge, was a small jetty where my father kept his boat. It was from here that my mother, my sister Freda and I used to swim across the Canning to the Mount Henry side and back. In those days the river never failed to deliver a good feed of prawns and crabs to the keen fisherman.

(In his later life my father retired to Yunderup on the Murray River, where he built himself — with Langford's help and mine — a modest dwelling which became his home. He lived there in the 1950s from the age of 70 until he died at the age of 79. Mum joined him from time to time but she was a more social person and missed her friends in Perth.)

I suppose that by comparison with conditions and lifestyles of just one generation earlier, we were bathing in high technology. Our lives were being changed at an ever-increasing rate by the transport revolution (new modes of surface travel and air travel) and the communication revolution (radio and film). But of course, by comparison, just one generation later we would be seen to have been leading very simple and relatively uncomplicated lives. Our children could make the same assertion with conviction. A child nowadays could be described not as bathing but as wallowing in high tech.

CHAPTER 3
PRE-WAR, 1929–1939

My primary school days had come to a close when several from my class, including me, were awarded scholarships and entrances to Perth Modern School (PMS). This represented the culmination of our primary education and was the goal to which many of us aspired. Study and sport were the focus of this elite scholarship school, which had a staff of excellent, specially selected teachers. Anyone lucky enough to gain entrance to PMS had access to the best education in Perth.

Perth Modern School was located not far from where I lived although this time it was beyond reasonable walking distance; I needed a push bike to get there. It was a new educational experience and one which I took to readily. I made many friends and enjoyed the new subjects we were taught.

But the carefree life style of the 1920s quickly gave way to the Great Depression of the 1930s which followed the catastrophic collapse of the New York Stock Exchange in 1929. The countries hardest hit were the primary producers and Australia took a hard blow. By 1933 one-third of Australia's workforce was out of a job and the dole queues grew longer and longer.

The Depression did not hit the Kerrs of Northwood Street at first and our standard of living did not suffer greatly, but in 1935 the axe dropped and my father lost his comfortable job. The American company he worked for sacked all its Australian managers and replaced them with Americans.

He came home one day to inform us. After we had digested the bad news he took me aside and said, 'Alex, I'm afraid you'll have to give up Modern School and look for some work. My income has suddenly taken a dive.' It was a severe jolt, particularly since I liked my school so much. But I was aware of the seriousness of the situation and after some moments, when I had gathered my thoughts, I commiserated with Dad over his loss and said, 'Well, bad luck. But I'll start looking right away.'

I spent that night thinking about the drastic changes that this would make to my life. I was half sorry about losing my chance to complete my education but equally excited about what may be in store for me in the world of business. My inbuilt sense of optimism always stood me in good stead at times like this when there was a change of fortune.

So I went from Perth Modern School to WA Newspapers as an office boy in early 1936. It was somewhat of a different start from that which I had built up in my mind as the beginning of the promising career of Alex Kerr, writer and international adventurer par excellence! Nevertheless, this was another new experience and another very pleasurable and important segment of my life. I matured quickly and tasted many new facets of life as a working youth. I made many new friends and tried my hand at a lot of new activities. I settled into the staff of the *Western Mail*, the weekly journal for country people which was produced in the offices of *The West Australian*.

Here, among other things, I organised a library for country readers, each week trundling a trolley loaded with brown paper parcels of books along William Street to the Roe Street section of the Railways parcel post. There I dispatched the current orders to all parts of the state (I soon became familiar with the names of all the Western Australian country towns) and picked up the parcels of returns from the grateful readers. There was no charge for this service. I shared a room with Mary Durack, who ran the women's section and wrote under the pseudonym of 'Virgilia', and Jack Mallett, who wrote the farmers' section under the pseudonym of 'Martingale'.

In a room at the rear of the Newspaper establishment worked Clive Gordon, cartoonist for the *West* and for the *Broadcaster*, the weekly newspaper for radio programs. Clive also drew the weather map each day from a chart which I used to pick up daily from the weather bureau. In those days the observatory, which housed the weather bureau, was located at the top of St George's Terrace, opposite the entrance to King's Park, and I used to catch a parlour car outside Newspaper House to travel up the hill to the observatory. The parlour cars were large lumbering vehicles which can best be described as a cross between a sedan car and a bus. They were not successful as a means of mass transit and soon vanished from the scene. When I see reference to today's lightning electronic means of communication my mind slips back to the image of a young lad sitting in the lumbering parlour car with an envelope on his lap containing a piece of paper on which is drawn the daily weather map.

I established a film section in the *West* and used to apply regularly to the film companies for 'stills' to be used for publication in my column. In this way I built up quite a library of black and white photographs of the film stars of those days. My desire to be a journalist had another outlet in my writing occasional articles which were published from time to time in the *West* Saturday literary section and occasional short stories, most of which were not accepted for publication anywhere, and a few songs which no-one but me ever listened to.

To complete my studies at Junior and Leaving Certificate level, I took night courses at Perth Technical College in the Terrace. I had enrolled for these immediately upon leaving school. I was able, in that way, to finish my Junior Certificate without losing ground and to complete my Leaving Certificate in two years, thus enabling me to go to university in 1939. I enrolled for a Diploma in Journalism — a course which was offered pre-war — and attended for the first two terms, but the war intervened and I never did finish it. It was not offered post-war.

Almost as an aftermath of the Great Depression, but with roots going far back in history, war clouds began gathering over Europe from the mid-1930s onwards and life became less effervescent and more sombre.

In 1936 the 16th Battalion Cameron Highlanders of Western Australia was formed as a rebirth of the 16th Battalion AIF, a Western Australian Infantry Battalion which had distinguished itself in World War I. The army barracks in Francis Street, Perth, became its headquarters for a short time. Together with my friend from WA, Tom Nisbet, I joined up in November of that year. I had to put up my age by two years before the recruiting sergeant would sign the papers. Eighteen months later I had my sergeant's stripes.

Bret Langridge also joined the battalion at that time as did Frank Sublet. Captain Bret Langridge was subsequently killed on the Kokoda Track but Frank and Tom both went on to command the battalion. After the war, coincidentally, I married Bret's sister Joan.

Those years in the 16th Battalion were for me a period of development in a different direction. They were years in which my friends and I developed self-confidence and leadership and learned what comradeship and being part of a team meant. Camps at Rottnest, Guildford and Northam and weekend bivouacs in the country at selected sites and weekends at the Swanbourne rifle range provided healthy, invigorating and exciting outdoor activities and gave us proficiency in map-reading, communications, team work, self-reliance, survival techniques and weapon training. I enjoyed using the .303 rifle at Swanbourne and became company-shot of B Company, for which I was awarded the silver crossed rifles to wear on my sleeve.

Our social life was full-on. In the winter we went to many dances and social outings. Tom and I used to frequent the Embassy Ballroom in Perth on Saturday nights, finishing the evening by walking home together to West Leederville and Shenton Park, stopping the milkman on the way to purchase a bottle of milk each.

As a budding young reporter, I used to spend my winter Saturday afternoons visiting local sporting games (hockey and football), writing down final scores and game highlights to phone in to the *West* for publication Monday morning. It brought in a small income but was not a very pleasant way of spending the time, especially on some of those cold rainy afternoons. But it did get me known by the subeditors and it paid off when Gubby Allen's England test team came to Australia in 1938 for what was to be the last ashes series for some years.

I was given the delightful task of attending the WACA ground each day of the England–Western Australia match and phoning through the scores every hour to 6IX, the WA Newspapers radio station. With my pass to the ground, I used to turn up early, dressed in whites, and practise at the nets bowling to the English players, who were a delightful bunch of chaps. The peak of my most undistinguished cricket career was when I clean bowled the great Walter Hammond in the nets. I was walking on air for days. Upon mature reflection and with the sobering effect of the passage of time, I soon came to the conviction that Hammond had deliberately missed that ball in order to give the Aussie kid something to brag about. I was seventeen at the time.

Then there was the Newspaper Rascals Harmonica Band. In 1938 I set that up with a few friends. We used to practise at night in the Newspaper House lunch room. It grew over time to become a respectable band, even going to air one night with a recital over 6IX. We had a formidable array of specialised mouth organs, from the top of the range Hohner chromatica, which we were all capable of playing, to bulky bass harmonicas and long alto harmonicas, all obtained from the proceeds of the raffle that I ran each Friday (pay day). Friday lunchtime I would buy a Van Heusen shirt and a tie from Walsh's in Hay Street and then wrap the prize attractively in cellophane. The linotype operators in the composing room at Newspaper House would run off for me ruled sheets for the entry of names and I would then do the rounds from department to department selling tickets in the raffle. We did not make much on one single shirt but after several weeks we would have sufficient money to buy another specialised instrument. In this way we built up our impressive range of instruments.

I had three main sporting activities at that time — cricket in summer and baseball and hockey in the winter. The cricket I played in the matting league as a member of the WA Newspapers team. The hockey I played for Old Modernians for one season only. The baseball I played for Wests Baseball Club, a club sponsored by *The West Australian*. This became my main sport and in fact was the only sport in which I could say I was reasonably good.

Apart from the WA Baseball League games, which were between clubs formed on a geographical district basis and always played on a Sunday, there grew up (encouraged by C.P. Smith, Managing Editor of *The West Australian* and a great aficionado of the game) another league which was known as the lunchtime league or the newspaper league. Games between the 'Wests' and the 'Press' were played each Tuesday and Thursday at lunchtime on The Esplanade at the foot of William Street and used to attract good crowds as the Perth public began to learn the ins and outs of this new game.

Although I got as far as the state trials my baseball days were cut short by the war, but my interest in the game carried forward to POW camps. There I formed an Australian team in Stalag Luft VI to play an American team from the next compound. After the war I founded the University Baseball Club, an action which ultimately earned me a University Blue. When I left WA for Canberra in 1950, we had two teams in the competition. When I returned in 1952 the club was fielding four teams in four different grades. I subsequently was asked to become patron of the club and then became the club's first life member.

In 1949 we had a bevy of student players who were later to find fame and fortune in disparate spheres of activity but who had at least their love of the game in common: Bob Hawke, Rolf Harris, Lawrie Sawle, several interstate cricketers and one all-Australian hockey player were in my early teams.

Alas our great pre-war times were to end rather abruptly with the declaration of war by Great Britain and the Commonwealth countries in late 1939 and the disastrous defeat of the Allied armies in Europe by Germany in 1940, leading to the withdrawal of Allied forces at Dunkirk. From late 1939 Tom and I were fulltime in the army. Tom was to remain in the army, rising to the rank of brigadier, while I transferred to the air force, eventually rising to the rank of warrant officer.

CHAPTER 4
OFF TO WAR, 1940

Soon after the fateful declaration of war came in September 1939, I left the *West* with a heavy heart. I had enjoyed those years so much and I took with me a fine monogrammed Cameron Tartan rug, which had been presented to me by the newspaper staff. I carried it with me on all my air force travels and I still have it to this day. My departure was leavened with a sense of excitement and anticipation.

Upon the declaration of war I was called up by the army, and the 16th Battalion encamped immediately on Rottnest for a fortnight of training and exercises. A three-month army camp at Northam followed. Here we prepared to go to war. I was by now platoon sergeant of 5 Platoon in B company.

Unbeknown to my senior officers and colleagues in the army, I had earlier (when I was 17) applied for a short service commission in the RAAF. For as long as I can remember it had been my ambition to become a pilot. As a small boy I had been taken by my brother to see a visiting Klemm monoplane land on a grass field at Jolimont and from that moment on I was hooked on flying. I learnt about every aircraft that had been flown by the RAF and the Luftwaffe since their inception and of the aces that had flown in them, and avidly read the books of W.E. Johns and the other few authors who wrote about flying in those days. But I had given up hope of making it to the air force and threw myself into army life with vigour and enthusiasm.

Imagine my surprise when my commanding officer at Northam had me paraded one morning in April 1940 to tell me that Air Board had called me up! He was not happy about losing a trainee officer, but I was over the moon. It subsequently became clear that with the passage of time and the arrival of my eighteenth birthday I had progressed to the top of the list to be called up for a short service commission. But that scheme was jettisoned and the Empire Air

Training Scheme (EATS) established in its place. Consequently I was first on the call-up list for that.

We were officially enlisted on 27 April 1940, after a medical examination and other formalities including IQ tests. Along with other inductees from other states we became No. 1 intake, EATS. The newly enlisted airmen became trainee pilots, navigators and wireless operators.

At last my long desire to become a fighter pilot seemed to become a possibility. The EATS recruited aircrew trainees from all parts of the British Empire to be trained in remote parts of the 'Empire' which were safe from foul weather and enemy action, and then sent them to the operational zones.

As I was leaving, Mr Blair, my best friend's father, who was a pilot in the Australian Flying Corps in World War I, said to me, 'Alex, as you know during the war I was a captain in the 11th Battalion and towards the end of the war I transferred to the AFC (Australian Flying Corps) because it seemed more exciting. I was trained to fly a Sopwith Pup and fell in love with flying. The war ended shortly after I started flying. I kept my 'wings' and still have them. I'd like you to have them for good luck.' He extended his hand with the precious AFC brevet in it. I was overwhelmed by his generosity and determined to treat them with great respect.

After a round of parties and fond farewells, on 27 April 1940, along with a bunch of other would-be aircrew, I was bundled into a truck in St George's Terrace and then transferred to an interstate train at the Perth Railway Station. From here it was a slow and very cramped trip across the Nullarbor. We were apprehensive and excited, trying to imagine what lay ahead, as our train steamed eastward over the desolate and dusty plain on our way to our first destination.

In the same truck as me was Selwyn Clark, who had also been in the Cameron Highlanders prior to joining the RAAF. Unknown to us, that meeting in the truck was to become the start of a lifelong friendship that lasted to the end. Sel, as he became known, was posted to an air gunner's school in Ballarat, but he was determined to become a pilot and when he topped his exams at Ballarat he was transferred to the pilots course and rejoined me. He was a good pilot, as he demonstrated later, and was of a hail-fellow-well-met temperament. With his ukelele, which he took around the world with him, he was the life and soul of any party. He carried his bonhomie and his ukelele with him for the rest of his life.

Our first destination was our Initial Training School at Somers in Victoria. This was the first of four stages in our training for aircrew, the first two of which were carried out in Australia. The third was in Canada and the fourth in Scotland.

Previously a well-appointed Boy Scouts camp, Somers had been modified to accommodate 40 new air force recruits and was now fully functioning as an Air Force Training School under the command of Squadron Leader Thomas White, who was later knighted and appointed Australian High Commissioner in London. A dapper little man with a DFC from service in the Australian Flying Corps in World War I, he ran the school smoothly and well and he rapidly won the respect of his charges. (I looked him up in Parliament House, Canberra, after the war, when he was Minister for Air in the Menzies government, and we reminisced wistfully about the 'early days', before things got tough).

The two-month course covered the basics: mathematics, navigation, meteorology, air frames, aeronautics, theory of flight, engine maintenance and all the things that a budding pilot should have some inkling of before taking to the skies. This was interspersed with route marches, parade ground drill, sport afternoons, when we challenged the nearby Flinders naval station to football and rugby, and delightful weekends when we frequented the best Melbourne dance halls in the company of a group of lovely girls who had been rounded up by my cousin, Pat Turnbull, to help the war effort. Having Pat and her mother and father there was a godsend for those West Australians amongst us and provided a most appreciated relief from the weekly concentrated study for me and my friends.

In July, having completed the Initial Training Course, we were posted from Somers to various functioning aerodromes to enter the second stage of our training — Elementary Flying Training School. Sel and I were posted to Mascot while the bulk of the graduates were posted to Narromine. Our social group broke up and we said our fond farewells to the girls who had made our weekends so enjoyable. Upon arriving at Mascot I found that I and three others had been posted to No. 2 flight at Newcastle aerodrome while Sel was posted to No. 3 flight at Mascot proper. And so we began the serious business of flying.

My instructors were Buddy Myers, who later became a much respected Qantas pilot, and Chris Burlace, who was the chief instructor at the flying club. It was not long before I was sitting on the green flying field waiting to take off for my first experience of flying. My first flight in a Tiger Moth! What a long-awaited and long-dreamed-of thrill. It was exciting and exhilarating and I knew right away, as we sped over the grass and finally quit our contact with the earth, that this was the life for me.

I soloed at just under five hours, which was considered excellent and no doubt helped later when 40 trainees were selected to go to Canada for advanced training. We were required to be efficient in take-offs and landings, of course, and also in forced landings, navigation, loops, slow rolls to both sides, blind spins (with a hood over our heads), side slipping and stalling. The instructors were efficient and patient. Once we soloed we were sometimes given freedom to take the aircraft up on our own and fly into the hinterland to practise all the things we had been taught. It was a wonderful feeling to be up there completely on your own with a delightful little aircraft which would take you wherever you told it to go. I traced figures of eight around trees on the inland farms, chased the outlines of cumulous clouds, practised side-slipping almost to the ground, constantly practised slow rolls — I felt the delightful little aircraft was a part of me.

While at Newcastle we made female friends — I palled up with Betty Rushbrooke, whose father was the officer in command of the Newcastle flight. Blonde, vivacious, fun-loving Betty lightened up my short time in Newcastle. As a group, with our girlfriends, we made several sorties to Sydney and tasted the atmosphere of Sydney's two most upmarket night clubs — Princes and Romanos. It was a new experience for us — Perth had nothing to match the attractions of Sydney's night life. We also managed a quick look at some of Sydney's historic sites. What a wonderful carefree life we lived, not to be equalled at any other stage of our training, which became more serious as we neared the theatre of operations.

But our flying delights soon came to an end and we were recalled to Mascot where the four best Mascot pilots were selected to join 36 others from Narromine to go to Ottawa for advanced fighter training on North American Harvards. The selection process was to take the highest rated pilot from each of the four flights at Mascot. I won top place for the Newcastle flight and the other three top pilots were Sel and Ken Hicks from Western Australia, and Monty Cotton from NSW. (For the subsequent record, Ken was killed in action in his second week of operations, I was shot down and taken prisoner in my third week of operations and, of the two who survived the war, Sel retired as a flight lieutenant with a Distinguished Flying Cross (DFC), and Monty retired as a squadron leader with a DFC).

We were all given pre-embarkation leave and for Sel, Ken and I that meant a train trip across the Nullarbor, followed by parties, family farewells and a trip across the Nullarbor again. On my way through the train stopped at Kellerberrin in the middle of the night, where to my surprise my lifelong friend Bob Blair was waiting to farewell me. I appreciated the gesture. Unfortunately that was the last time I saw Bob; later he gave his life as a bomber pilot over Europe.

Once back together again we were assembled at Sydney's Circular Quay and embarked on the motor vessel *Awatea,* a recently commissioned New Zealand ship of 20,000 tons. The embarkation process was a government PR exercise from start to finish. Banks of movie cameras and radio microphones homed in on us as we were farewelled by the Minister for Air and the top air force brass. There were several speeches and several long photograph poses both on and off the ship. It was obvious that we were to become the focus of a lot of publicity throughout Australia. Eventually the ceremonies died down and we were all mustered on board. Sel with his ukelele, and Ken, Monty and I, now and henceforth known as the Four Mascoteers, sang 'Please don't talk about me when I'm gone'.

As the *Awatea* pulled away from the quay I couldn't help wondering when or whether I would ever set foot on Australian soil again.

CHAPTER 5

THE PACIFIC AND CANADA, 1940

After a short trip to New Zealand where we met the mayor of Auckland, local dignitaries and the senior officers of the New Zealand Air Force, and where we were treated to a lightning tour of Auckland and its major tourist attractions, we set off eastwards across the Pacific. Little did we know that the friendly and lavish treatment we received in Auckland was but a foretaste of what was to come in all our ports of call until we reached war-torn England.

Making good time across the Pacific (the *Awatea* was a new and speedy passenger vessel) we were kept busy aboard our luxurious accommodation with sessions of mathematics, theory of flight, navigation, morse code, meteorology and other studies. The food and entertainment aboard were first class and we were really pampered for two weeks or so. The routine was broken only twice; first at Fiji, where we were given shore leave, and then in Hawaii.

Suva was fascinating. Many of us for the first time experienced handicrafts and fresh fruit at the street markets and the local drink, kava, which we found so earthy. Sel and I were particularly intrigued by the island music and we had one session in our cabin when several lumpers from the wharf borrowed Sel's ukulele and sang several island songs in wonderful harmony. Our favourite was 'Isa Lei'.

Hawaii was a somewhat different experience. As we were not allowed ashore some kind official had arranged for a troupe of hula dancers to come aboard to entertain us. This they did for several hours with their singing and dancing. More ukuleles and guitars introduced us to the haunting music of the islands. We learned many of their songs and the melodies lingered in our memories forever.

Chapter 5

Vancouver greeted us with a brass band on the wharf and dozens of movie cameras as we gently docked to the cheers of the waiting crowd. Badges of office, gold braid and medals added colour to the welcoming spectacle. A fleet of black limousines was lined up in the main street and as we disembarked we were driven to the majestic Vancouver Hotel where the mayor gave us an official welcome luncheon on the fourteenth floor (Canadian salmon was the main course!). This was just a prelude to our reception wherever we went until we arrived, after a long and wonderful trip on the Canadian Pacific Railway through the Rockies, at our destination — Ottawa.

After the official welcome in Vancouver we were given three days' leave to see the city and meet the people. Everywhere we were warmly welcomed and if we walked into a hotel bar there was no way anyone would allow us to buy a drink. We took in as much of the beautiful city as we could in three short days, Sel and I remarking on how similar it was to our hometown, Perth. Years later I visited and stayed in Vancouver several times and each time my thoughts went back to that group of young, eager would-be pilots, off to see the world.

The time came to board the impressive Canadian Pacific Railway and begin to make our way eastward across the continent, first taking in the Rockies. We sped past those majestic snow-covered mountains drinking in the breath-taking scenery. At every stop we were greeted by batteries of cameras and microphones and we began to realise what an important public relations exercise this was. Britain was thirsting for pilots after the attrition of the Battle for Britain and each Commonwealth country was doing its best to plug the gap. These early propaganda efforts were no doubt made to increase the rate of volunteering.

Finally we arrived in Ottawa. Here we were welcomed by the Australian Liaison Officer, Air Vice-Marshal Goble, and installed in the air force base at Uplands, on the outskirts of the city.

It was not long before we were immersed in all aspects of our training, at a frenetic pace. The aircrew quarters at Uplands, the Ottawa airport where we carried out our flying training, were quite comfortable but outside our barracks the weather was not very friendly. Winter was setting in and most of our training was in snow, with temperatures later dropping to −20 degrees Fahrenheit. I spent four days in hospital with frostbitten feet at the height of the cold spell, despite the cumbersome flying boots I wore when flying. Our cockpits were not heated.

We began our flying training on Yale aircraft, a single radial-engine monoplane which was quite user friendly, although fairly slow. From the Yales we soon graduated to North American Harvards, which were much more sophisticated and boasted a much more powerful radial engine and a greater speed. They were also harder to fly. They were used as operational fighter aircraft in the Pacific theatre of war. It was on the Harvards that we learnt all the basic skills for fighter pilots in the third stage of our training — the Intermediate Flying Training School — and finally qualified for our flying brevets, or 'wings'. These were presented to us at the wings parade in early December, amid pomp and splendour and much gold braid, on a snow-covered parade ground. We felt very proud to have our wings sewn on to our tunics at last.

Our social life was not lacking. Shortly after we arrived in Ottawa the Australian High Commissioner, Sir William Glascow, threw a welcome party to which he had invited 40 Ottawa girls who were about our age. We soon palled up with them and some of the airmen, including myself and Selwyn, made lasting friends. On weekends we were invited to our friends' homes to sleep over, and parties and dances were arranged for the whole time we were there. More than once we dined at the majestic Hotel Laurier and danced to their big band just as Glen Miller's 'In the Mood' was becoming popular. My friend was Alison Cochrane, a petite fun-loving brunette whose father, Farrer Cochrane, was Canadian Surveyor-General. I was made to feel one of the family and had a wonderful time staying with them. Our highlight was skiing in the streets of Ottawa at night on the occasions when the snow was suitable.

Within two weeks of graduating, our good life ended and we found ourselves in a rusted old freighter — the S.S. *Pennland* — ploughing, protesting, through a fierce Atlantic storm in company with many other ships in a large convoy. It made its weary way across the Atlantic to Britain. We were protected from the predatory and ubiquitous German U-Boats by a fleet of destroyers weaving in and out of the convoy but, even so, one of our ships was sunk en-route. Monty Cotton and I, having had several years in the army, had volunteered to man a Lewis gun mounted on the upper deck but we had no occasion to use it as the possibility of air attack was remote.

The conditions on the *Pennland* were appalling — below decks, soiled and slippery with vomit, sick soldiers and airmen were prostrated everywhere, not caring whether the ship was torpedoed or not. The rusty vessel creaked and groaned its miserable way across the angry and forbidding ocean, eventually to dock in Liverpool on 13 December 1940. (As an aside, by a great coincidence, I chanced to glance at a short note in *The West Australian*, circa 1947, which announced that the *Pennland* had broken up and sunk in the mid-Atlantic! Given its condition when we sailed in it, I was not surprised.) We were a sorry lot when we made our landfall at Liverpool.

With a day to clean ourselves up in port, we were officially welcomed to Britain next day, lined up on the deck of our decrepit old hulk, by the Duke of Hamilton on 14 December. He spoke briefly under a leaden sky and we were then marshalled for our train ride to London. We hoisted our large kitbags onto our shoulders and prepared to enter a new phase in our lives.

CHAPTER 6
ENGLAND AT WAR, 1941

By this time the Battle for Britain in the skies had been fought and won by the RAF, at great cost in pilots' lives, prompting Churchill's famous tribute 'Never was so much owed by so many to so few'. The planned invasion was clearly now impossible. Hitler's plans, and Goering's, had been rudely jolted and the first stage of the German air offensive, which had been planned to destroy Britain's air defences, had failed. It now entered its second stage — the night bombing of Britain. We were soon to experience it first hand. After being fitted out with flying gear at Uxbridge and assigned to various RAF squadrons (there were no RAAF squadrons in Britain as yet, apart from No. 10 Sunderland flying boat squadron) we were given a few days' leave before making our way to the various operational training units to which we had been posted.

Not knowing anyone in England we took our leave in London, which by now was becoming heavily bombarded by night. Sel and I would stand wearing our tin helmets and listening to the pitter-patter of anti-aircraft shrapnel as it fell out of the skies. We were constantly reminded that what goes up must come down! The bombardment took place to the haunting accompaniment of the wailing air raid sirens and the constant thump-thump of the bombs falling. The Germans had taken to dropping thousands of incendiary bombs as well as high explosives and over the Christmas and New Year period of 1940 London was consumed by fire in what became known as the Second Great Fire of London. The heroic auxiliary fire fighters spent each night trying to douse the flames with leaky hoses and to rescue people from the ruins of their houses, at great risk to themselves. Sirens rarely gave up their wailing and through the night ambulances with just a slit for headlights raced here and there, contributing their own wailing, to give succour to the injured.

Chapter 6

On New Year's Eve, Sel and I stood on Tower Hill and in all directions we could see London ablaze as the bombers droned overhead. At night most of the population sought refuge in the underground railway stations dotted around London. Heading for our hotel we would descend into the Underground, get used to the pervading smell of sweat and food, and pick our way across the inert sleeping bodies of the families who had taken to spending their nights in the safety of the tunnels.

We had bought a baby Austin for 10 pounds and during the day we drove around to see what we could of London by daylight, picking our way through leaky fire hoses and the squads of army and police personnel and the piles of debris on the roads. It was, indeed, a sorry sight. The only thing that seemed not to be damaged was the spirit of the Londoners. The war was well and truly biting into their lifestyles, with the nightly blackouts, food and petrol and clothing rationing, but they still carried on as best they could under the circumstances. Australia House was a focal point for our activities, the Queen's Brasserie was a favourite watering place and the newly opened Windmill Theatre in Soho proved to be a major attraction.

Our leave was soon up and, bidding farewell to Sel and the other friends with whom I had trained, I set off by myself for Lossiemouth, an operational training unit north of Edinburgh, near Inverness. I was feeling miserable because I had been allotted to bombers whereas I had been trained for fighters. I was not then aware that, with the Battle of Britain over, the demand was now for bomber pilots to give back to the Germans what they had been dishing out to the British. Even so, it was another two years before the British bomber offensive was strong enough materially to affect the German war machine. But the payment was to be heavy.

Bomber Command earned for itself an unenviable reputation as the most dangerous unit of the Allied Armed Forces. Chances of remaining unhurt for more than a few weeks on operations were slim. Of the 125,000 aircrew of Bomber Command there were 76,000 casualties during the war. When the Americans came into the war their casualties were even more horrific. They concentrated on daylight bombing while the British concentrated on night bombing. I was not aware of these statistics when bound for Lossiemouth and perhaps that was just as well.

We were now in the fourth and final stage of our training — from ITS at Somers to EFTS at Mascot to ATS at Uplands to Operational Flying Training Unit (OTU) at Lossiemouth. Soon we would be operational.

Lossiemouth really had nothing to commend it in my view. The weather was foul and unpredictable, a far cry from the beautiful clear skies we had had in Australia and Canada. It was bitterly cold and we were freezing when we flew on training flights, despite the woollen underclothes and the heavy leather flying suits we wore. Most of the time, we walked around the aerodrome in the muddy slush of melting snow. We were close enough to the French coast for German night bombers to attack us, which they did from time to time.

On the first night I was there, our welcome to Lossiemouth took the form of a stick of bombs donated by a German night bomber which flew over our aerodrome at low level. I was in the mess and as the first one landed, followed instantly by the second and then the third, I guessed what was happening and was the first to dive under the mess table. I ended up with several bodies on top of me! There was no injury to personnel but the runway was damaged. When we flew on training flights at night we were vulnerable to marauding German night fighters which had enough fuel to slip over to Scotland, look for an easy unsuspecting target and fly back before their fuel gave out. It wasn't long before we had our first casualty. Early one morning after a night training exercise, Alan McSweyn woke us up with the news that one of our Australian pilots, Eric McLeod, had been shot down by a night fighter. We realised that now we were well and truly in an operational area! Eric never got to fly on operations. He was one of the thousands of aircrew killed in training — mostly due to bad weather.

We heaved a sigh of relief when our operational training was completed. We packed up our kit and headed for our new squadron. We had not had much social life on OTU. The weather was against it, for one thing, and we were not near a large town that could provide a range of attractions. Elgin was the only town of any consequence for some miles around and it really did not have much to offer except one or two Saturday night dances which were very small and usually not well attended because of the inclement weather. I made contact with the local Presbyterian minister and visited him once or twice. I don't think any of the aircrews at Lossiemouth were sad at leaving when the time came. About the most exciting thing, before we were posted to different squadrons, was the night of our passing-out dinner when, after we had finished all the wine, and with the permission of our station medical officer, we ate all the flowers arranged nicely on vases around the festive tables.

We had been assigned to fly Wellingtons — twin-engine bombers — which we had trained on at OTU. The Wellington, or Wimpy as it was called, was a good aircraft, easy to fly and strong, and because of its geodetic construction it could take a good pounding from enemy anti-aircraft fire and still remain flying. Its one drawback was a reputation for burning rapidly and fiercely when set alight. It had a crew of six: two pilots, a navigator, two air-gunners and a wireless operator.

Two nights after we arrived and installed ourselves in our allotted accommodation, we all congregated in the mess hut and formed our crews from the 72 aircrew assembled there (six per aircraft). We were all in the dark, having never met before and it was rather a haphazard choice as we assembled behind the experienced captain of our choice. Then we set to for some serious training. I was the only Australian in our crew; the other five were British. John Anderson, who already had experience on several bombing raids, was the captain and I was the second pilot. Our navigator was Bill Legg, our wireless operator was Geoff Hogg, our front gunner was Bernie Morgan and our rear gunner was Dave Fraser.

Training was not pleasant as the weather was foul, and we lost another aircraft in training. It crashed and exploded into a fireball when returning from daytime bombing practice. Our training trips were focused on bombing practice, air-to-air target shooting, navigation and basic flying drills and we fitted them in, weather permitting. We were now into spring and the weather was improving.

Before we left Lossiemouth I had made contact with Sel, now known as 'Nobby', who had been posted to Sutton Bridge for OTU training on Hurricanes. We arranged that we would meet, together with Ken

Hicks, in London on our first leave and we were looking forward to exchanging experiences — the first three Western Australians EATS pilots. We had planned our few days together on our first operational leave. That meeting never took place: Ken, who had trained on Hurricanes, was shot down over the British Channel and killed and I was shot down over Germany. Sel found himself immediately bereft of friends. It was not an auspicious start to our wartime careers!

CHAPTER 7
ON OPERATIONS, 1941

We completed our training in April and were posted to 115 Squadron in Marham, Norfolk on 16 April 1941. After Lossiemouth we were glad to make the acquaintance of our new home in Norfolk. It was a pre-war permanent RAF station so the accommodation was quite good and with spring approaching the weather began to improve.

Life on the operational station was different from that on the training station. We had a better social life, being in a more highly populated area with London not far away, so any leave could offer more alternatives. Saturday night dances were always a great attraction if we weren't on operations, and the townships provided a good variety of restaurants, live theatre and films for diversion from the strains of operational flying.

As crews chalked up more and more trips the strain began to show and those lucky enough to complete a tour (30 operations) were usually in need of a substantial period of leave to recover before they were required to resume operations. Some unlucky ones, who crumbled under the continual pressure of night after night with their lives up for grabs, finally refused to fly anymore. They were unkindly classified as LMF (lack of moral fibre), had their rank and flying brevets taken from them and were given ground jobs in disgrace. I think that this unsympathetic treatment of personnel who, for various understandable reasons, could not stand up to the pressure, was abandoned towards the end of the war.

Training on squadron was more of the routine we had at Lossiemouth, particularly bombing and navigation and air-to-air firing, and it was not long before we were assembled for our first operational briefing on the afternoon of 25 April 1941. I had just celebrated my twentieth birthday two days before.

We assembled in the crew room and Wing Commander Marwood Elton traced our chosen course on a large map which designated our target for the night. It was the dock area in Emden and was considered by the experienced captains to be a relatively 'soft' target. This was comforting to the newcomers, who by this time were experiencing feelings of excitement mixed with premonition and uncertainty about how they would react to the flak and fighters.

Following the briefing came the individual preparations of each crew member. I took the AFC wings that Mr Blair had given me when I left Perth and sewed them onto the outside of my thick flying jacket as a good luck token. They remained there until the night of my last operation.

Then we were into the truck to take us out to dispersal where our Wellington was waiting for us. We waddled (with our several layers of clothing and our leather trousers and jacket we all looked fat and unwieldy) over to the dark sinister shape, carrying our parachutes and helmets. The aircraft was being bombed up and maintenance mechanics were scurrying here and there, testing external controls, as we climbed up the ladder to the entry hatch of the aircraft.

Andy was at the ladder giving orders: 'You first, Bernie – first in, last out.'

'I don't think I like that.'

'You'll be right. Now Alex then me into the cockpit.'

Dave called, 'Hey, Bill! What are you doing?'

'I'm pissing on the tyre.'

'What for?'

'Good luck.'

'What kind of luck is that? I hope the rubber holds out till we get back to land on it. Now get inside.'

'She'll be right, mate.' Bill zippered several layers of clothing and climbed up the ladder.

Dave Fraser was the last in. As he wriggled his way awkwardly into his confined gun turret he turned and shouted: 'See you in about seven hours, chaps!'

Bernie Morgan crawled into his place in the front gun turret and began to make himself as comfortable as he could in the cramped space that was to contain him for the next six hours lying on his stomach.

Chapter 7

Geoff Hogg settled into his seat at the radio compartment and began to tune his radio and check frequencies. Bill Legg settled at his table opposite Geoff and spread out his maps and began plotting our course. Dave Fraser climbed into the rear gun turret and began testing the hydraulics and ensuring the guns turned easily. Andy, the captain, and I, the second pilot, took our seats in the cockpit. When Andy started the engines we began to read and test the many gauges we had in front of us.

Chocks away! Throttles forward and with the two Pratt and Whitney engines straining their utmost, we began to lumber along with increasing speed, which never seemed to be enough to get us off the ground. Eventually we cleared the end of the dimly lit runway and climbed slowly up into the night. For the next eight hours we would be on our own flying, for the most part, in silence. We flew into intermittent heavy cloud and we settled into our routine as we gained altitude over the Channel.

Andy and I were checking all the engine gauges to make sure everything was in order, and synchronising the engines and adjusting the controls of the flying surfaces. Bernie and Dave in their turrets checked that their guns were working correctly and fired a burst into the darkness to make sure the firing mechanism was in order. Geoff and Bill were busy at their tables, Geoff checking his frequencies and maintaining radio silence on the way to the target and Bill estimating wind drift and air speed and plotting our track to the target. No-one spoke as we concentrated on our tasks. The only noise was the drone of the two Pratt and Whitney engines.

As we drew near to the French coast we were greeted by sporadic flak from the German flak ships anchored in the Channel. It was our first taste of enemy fire. We first thought how pretty it was with coloured lights arcing over the sky in varied patterns, but soon we realised those bursts of fire were not friendly. They sprayed their deadly red hot pieces of steel over the sky.

The flak became heavier over the target area. What seemed like puffs of cloud but were really bursts of high explosive would suddenly appear in front of the aircraft to be followed immediately by the acrid smell of the explosion and a buffeting as our plane flew through the shock waves of the blast. Here and there an aircraft would keel over and spiral down in flames while its crew struggled to bail out and escape the inferno.

As we approached the target Bill clambered down and lay on his stomach in his bombing position and adjusted his bombsight. From that point on, until his bombs were gone, he was in control of the aircraft. He directed Andy in a zigzag path towards the Emden dock area. He called out, 'Bomb doors open!' and as I activated the bomb doors switch I called back, 'Bomb doors open'. Bill then brought Andy to a straight and level path. As we drew close to the target he still had command: 'Left, left, steady, right, steady, hold it, hold it … bombs gone!' At the 'bombs gone' signal Andy, in command again, banked the plane and headed for home.

Generally flak was heaviest over the target and it was often difficult for the pilot to maintain a straight and level course. This he had to do to enable the bomb aimer to get an accurate sighting of the target. The last minute or so of steady flying was the most hazardous as the aircraft was a sitting duck for an accurate flak gunner. Sometimes bomb aimers would not be satisfied that the plane was in the correct position for bomb release and would abort the run and ask the skipper to go round again. As it was highly dangerous to linger over the target area for longer than was necessary, decisions to go around again were always very unpopular. Aircrew, understandably, were always anxious to get away from the target area as soon as possible although the danger was not immediately over, because on the outskirts of the intense flak of the target area there was always the night fighter to contend with. They could not operate in close to the target area because they were in danger from their own flak.

The official record of the result of our bombing on that night states: '*Located and attacked target and dropped one stick, southwest to northeast. No results were seen. Bombing height 13,500ft.*' These results were made available to me many years later when my wife, Joan, and I were guests of 115 Squadron on one of our visits to England. The copies that were taken from their records and given to me on that occasion were very much appreciated because my flying log book had disappeared from my belongings when I was shot down, removing the only record of my flying career.

The flight home was uneventful. We touched down at Marham about 1 am, and went straight to debriefing. After that it was into the mess for bacon and eggs and hot coffee and then to bed. Thus ended my first sortie over enemy territory — 115 Squadron lost several planes that night but we were among the lucky ones.

Returning from a training flight two days later I had a lucky break. Coming in to land I followed the procedures laid down, including checking to see whether the green light on the instrument panel was glowing to show that the wheels were locked into the 'down' position. As I touched down the starboard wheel folded up, causing the aircraft to slew around. The port wheel, which was locked into position, collapsed from the lateral movement and the aircraft slid sideways down the runway, shuddering and screaming as it scraped the bitumen. The tips of both propellers were bent and both engines were emitting smoke. The sideways movement broke the wing and twisted the geodetic frame of the aircraft. It was a complete wipe-out.

Wellingtons had a bad reputation for blazing like a torch in these circumstances. For some unknown reason this one didn't. Fortunately my reflexes were working well and I had turned off both engine switches in a flash as I felt the aircraft going. Undoubtedly that helped to prevent the dreaded fire. As we slithered to a halt in a cloud of dust and debris, with a grinding, deafening rumble and the sound of breaking metal and hissing engines, the two experienced airmen with us were out of the escape hatch and running as fast as they could from the expected explosion. The fire never came; I and the flight-lieutenant instructor in the cockpit were lucky to walk away with our lives.

The squadron commander, Wing Commander Marwood-Elton, came speeding out in his jeep in a foul temper. He obviously assumed that I had forgotten to check my undercarriage lights before touchdown, a not uncommon error with new pilots. To him it meant the loss of one of his precious bombers. He climbed up on his jeep so that he was level with my face and through the window said, 'Kerr, I'll have you sent back to Australia for this.' In desperation I asked him to wait while I turned on the ignition. To my intense relief the green lights came on. It was a perfect vindication of my actions. We were victims of an electrical fault.

Our second target on 30 April was Kiel. This time the hostile reception we received was of greater intensity than on our first raid. We were deeper into Germany and when approaching the target had to watch for night fighters as well as searchlight cones.

By this time the German night fighter force was developing various techniques to combat the growing numbers of night bombers making incursions into their homeland. The searchlight operators had developed a system of 'coning' individual bombers so they could focus on one particular invader. When a single master searchlight locked on to an intruder, a cone of about 10 other searchlights forming part of a local system, linked electronically, would spring into life and all would focus on the one unfortunate aircraft. When this happened it was like daylight inside the cone. A night fighter would be zeroed on to the intruder by radio and would then attack from the darkness outside the cone of light. At this point, when flak stopped, you knew to look for a night fighter. Aircraft would dive and dodge in order to try to throw off the cone. Some were successful but many were not and the Bomber Command losses mounted. It was a cone that proved our undoing. Another tactic which was developed later by the night fighter force was to attack aircraft from below. Many aircraft were shot down in this way — shot out of the sky without knowing where the attack came from.

The squadron record of our sortie on this occasion states: *'Dropped one stick northwest to southeast close to Deutsche works. No bursts seen. Returned early owing to engine trouble. Bombing height 12,000 ft.'*

Our third operation on 3 May was Brest, where the German battleships *Scharnhorst* and *Gneisnau* were holed up, unable to put to sea because the British Navy had several capital ships which lay in waiting for them in the Channel. They were our targets. The flight across the Channel was uneventful but as we neared the target explosive shells from German flak ships began to burst around us. As we approached our objective the German defences grew in intensity; the two battleships were of great value to them. We could smell the cordite of the shells which filled the sky with their lethal shrapnel. We lined up for a bombing run (always the most hazardous of all due to the fact that the aircraft had to remain on a steady flight path in order to line up the target accurately) and after Bill signalled 'bombs gone' we twisted and turned and got away from the target area as quickly as we could.

On this occasion the record states: '*Located and attacked target. Bombed from 13,000 ft. Dropped a stick across quay east of river. One very large flash on edge of quay observed.*'

The flight back home was uneventful and as things quietened down we began to enjoy our Horlicks milk tablets and our chocolate bars and other sweets we had been issued with. Bernie, our front gunner, in his excitement used to eat his goodies while we were over the target, wrappers and all! Then came the welcome bacon and eggs to end our flight!

CHAPTER 8
A FIRE IN THE SKY, 1941

Andy had touched down on the grass airfield around midday 10 May 1941 in Wellington R1379 KO-B, having completed his air test. After taxiing to the dispersal point we all climbed down the ladder to wait for transport back to flight. Back at the flight he saw that instructions had been chalked on the board for the ground crew to fuel and bomb up our aircraft. It signified that we would be on operations that night after having volunteered to replace a crew that had experienced mechanical trouble with its aircraft. In the late afternoon we attended a briefing and learned that orders had come through from Bomber Command Headquarters for an attack on Hamburg.

One hundred and nineteen bombers were being despatched to bomb the general city area, the Altona power station, the shipyards and the nearby Blohm and Voss aircraft works. Sixty of these aircraft would be Wellingtons. Hampdens and Whitleys, and one Manchester, the forerunner of the Lancaster bomber, made up the complement. The designated target for KO-B was the dock area of Hamburg. Our take-off time was 22:17.

As we gathered our helmets and parachutes my attention was drawn to a flash of colour as the AFC wings sewn on my flying jacket fell to the floor. I had no time to reattach them so I carefully put them in my kitbag. Was that the end of my good luck?

It was a clear sky on the night of the 10th and our approach to the target had been fairly uneventful. But activity over the target area had been particularly brisk and we had received a sustained buffeting from the flak bursts but had still managed to maintain our course to the objective. Over the target fierce flak forced us off course and Bill aborted the bomb run forcing Andy to turn and to make another run. This second time Bill was able to release his bombs. We bombed the target in Hamburg, one of the most fiercely defended targets in

Chapter 8

Germany, and thankfully turned for home, though we were by no means out of the danger zone.

Puffs of grey smoke hung around us, seemingly motionless where their high explosive shells had burst, looking for all the world like a closely woven balloon barrage in some degree of confusion. Streams of coloured tracer spread backwards from the guns far below and curved over one another in graceful criss-crosses, forming a continuous lethal colourful display such as one would expect to find on a gala night in peacetime. Tonight had great significance for us but not as a festive occasion, as we were soon to discover.

I had not so far experienced fear on any of my raids — apprehension, perhaps, but not fear — a fact which struck me as rather strange but nevertheless very welcome. Upon later reflection, I realised that I had not yet been exposed to intense enemy fire for long enough to become scared. I was musing to myself. I remembered the previous raids when I had remarked to the rest of the crew how attractive the colourful streams of tracer looked from a distance. I was right there — from a distance. I had not yet seen them close and had not seen red hot shrapnel biting into the aircraft ripping metal and flesh and destroying everything it touched. Although there was always a good chance of it on each trip, I had not yet really been face to face with the high probability of death. No doubt that is why I had not yet experienced real fear.

My heart had missed a beat once or twice when we had received a particularly hard buffet from an uncomfortably close explosion, but that was all. I could easily think that we were in a severe electrical storm such as we had experienced in training and that the air turbulence which shook the aircraft was caused by natural rather than man-made disturbance. My thoughts wandered to those blinking, bluish searchlights far below, and the men who manned them. I could imagine them like minute ants, scurrying here and there shouting orders and whooping with grim delight when their beams of light picked up the dark outline of a night intruder.

The train of my thought was rudely broken by a sharp exclamation from Dave, the rear gunner — 'My turret's on fire, Andy.' There was no panic in his voice, only urgency. I didn't turn to look at the rear turret but kept my eyes on the searchlights, three of which had picked us up and held us, due no doubt to the fire in the rear gun turret which made a clear marker. Five seconds later our airspace became a blaze of light as a large cone of approximately 20 searchlights sprang into life and focussed on us. I felt Bill, the navigator, brush past me, extinguisher in hand, to assist Dave in attacking the fire. The flak had severed the hydraulic line that served the gun turret and set it on fire, immobilising it. Dave's voice rapped through the intercom once more, 'Night fighter on our tail.' My heart went into my throat as I realised that Dave could not use his guns to fight off the intruder! Caught in the cone of searchlights, rear turret on fire, night fighter on our tail, with our guns out of action we were a sitting duck. I hurriedly left my pilot's seat and ran to the centre of the aircraft where the transparent perspex astro-hatch was located. From there I could watch the intruder and let Andy know what was happening.

'Corkscrew right!' I shouted to Andy as I saw the dark shape looming up.

Twenty-seven-year-old night fighter Lieutenant Eckart-Wilhelm von Bonin of the 11/NJG 1, piloting a BF 110 twin-engine night fighter, had been vectored into the vicinity of the enemy aircraft. His task had been eased by the searchlights focussing on the Wellington bomber. He was now manoeuvring into position for an attack from the rear starboard quarter. This was his first operational interception. He was a new chum. He was keyed up and very apprehensive of the two guns in the rear turret of the bomber. Von Bonin would eventually become a highly decorated night fighter ace with 41 victories, but he was now to be tested in battle for the first time. Closing fast on the bomber he could not understand why the bomber's rear guns were not swinging in his direction. The enemy gunner, he thought, must have seen him by now. Tense, with the adrenaline pumping, he opened fire. Then he realised that only his machine guns were firing. In his excitement he had overlooked the firing button for the cannon that his aircraft was equipped with. It was a blessing in disguise for the Wellington crew, who would otherwise have been blown out of the sky! (These details became available 50 years later when von Bonin and I made personal contact and exchanged letters and experiences.)

The dark shape hovered expectantly and moved into position on the starboard quarter. I was aware of a tingling sensation at the back of my neck as I realised that we might have only a few more seconds! There was no time to lose. I rapped instructions to Andy for a quick turn and dive to starboard and felt the great plane starting to dip and swing round but it was too late. It was as light as day in that particular part of the sky and as we turned slowly I saw the fighter straighten up and could imagine him lining up the big bulk of our Wellington bomber for a sitting shot. We were completely helpless. As I watched he squeezed his trigger.

Fire spat from the fighter's wings and I saw the tracer bullets like fiery pinpoints flashing towards me. Many days later I wondered how many men who were shot were actually able to see the bullets hurrying towards their target as time stopped still. Before I could move I felt a heavy blow as though someone had punched me simultaneously all over my body. Later I learnt that I had taken seven bullets, in the chest, arm and leg. The bullets which ripped through the fabric and aluminium with a piercing noise knocked me backwards onto a canvas bed.

For a few seconds I was conscious. I had no idea where I was shot although I certainly knew that I had been hit and hit hard. At least I was still alive. I can remember feeling indignant that a German had actually had the nerve to shoot me and I cursed that pilot and his ancestors with all the heartfelt invective that I could muster. For those few seconds I also knew stark fear — the terrible fear of the helpless — as I could not move and yet barely two yards away a wild fire was raging. An incendiary bullet had ignited one of our flares inside the aircraft and it was burning fiercely with a bright yellow flame. During those few seconds of consciousness my imagination ran riot as I saw, in my mind's eye, hungry flames devouring my parachute harness then my leather flying suit, then me. The flames faded out as I lost consciousness.

There is no official bombing report. The squadron record simply states: '*Sgt Anderson and Sgt Kerr, missing as result of flying battle casualty on 10/11 May 1941.*'

I came to my senses some way down the aircraft by the rear escape hatch. My adrenaline had obviously gone into overdrive and given me the strength to rise up and get my body near the escape hatch. The flames were still there, even more intense, lighting up the interior of the fuselage with a great yellow glare, to the accompaniment of a loud crackling and hissing sound and the acrid smell of petrol and oil fumes. It was a huge, grim bonfire. The fear that had first gripped me was gone now and in its stead was a lulling, lethargic calm, a slowness of movement that could well be fatal in an emergency. I was just not thinking properly. I was sitting on the deck with the large well-built form of Dave, the rear gunner, hovering behind me, parachute in hand. My own chute was clipped to my chest. My movements were almost mechanical as if I were preoccupied, as if the stark reality of the situation was numbing my brain and preventing any action.

As my thinking became clearer, I checked my parachute, dangled my legs over the escape hatch then looked around me. The noise inside the aircraft was deafening and the interior well lit up. Perhaps the size of the flares was magnified in my eyes but it seemed to me that the entire forepart of the fuselage was afire. We were, I thought, a great flying torch. I saw the form of Bill, the navigator, half lying, half sitting near the astro-hatch, evidently hit by the same burst that had got me as we had been standing close to one another.

As I looked Bill stirred and turned towards me. So he was not dead. I endeavoured to beckon with my left hand but it would not function. I could see the leather sleeve of my flying jacket ripped open and lots of blood. I beckoned with my right hand and was answered with a shake of the head and a gesture which signified to me that he could not move. I turned back to Dave and tried to speak above the noise but no sound seemed to come from my lips. I looked down and could see my left leg and my torn leather flying suit trousers with bright red blood oozing out of the rip. It was also flowing down inside my trouser leg and trickling into my flying boot, warm and clammy.

Dave seemed not to be able to understand that I had difficulty moving my arms and legs. He smiled and beckoned me to jump. The flames were roaring with ferocious intensity and Dave was obviously getting impatient. Finally I felt Dave put my hand on my rip cord, yelling at me to pull the cord as he did so. A clip of my harness caught on something and Dave fumbled with it. Then a final shove did what my own limbs refused to do and sent me flying into the darkness.

I was whipped backwards by the airflow and lost no time in pulling the rip cord. The rustling of the silk pilot chute, the sharp report of the big canopy opening, a hard jolt on my shoulders and I knew I was safe for the moment. The flaming body of our plane was below descending, it seemed, at a great rate. I had a dim recollection of seeing two other parachutes floating slowly downwards and was startled by the dark roaring shape of an aeroplane which flashed past me, uncomfortably close. I remembered ripping off my flying helmet and goggles and flinging them away. Then all became quiet. The stillness which had descended on that area was undisturbed by flak or searchlights or the noise of aircraft. They had turned their attention elsewhere. In the blackness nothing happened to upset the gentle swishing sound made by the wind in the silken canopy above me. I felt myself dozing, floating, floating, gently, quietly.

Bump! A hard blow on my feet and then the back of my head heralded mother earth. It was a rude awakening from my reverie. I had dropped off to sleep, lulled by warm blood oozing into the palm of my hand and down my leg, and had lost all sense of height and time and location.

I heard voices and gave vent to a feeble call for help which was answered from nearby. I was lying on my back with the parachute dragging me along the rough ground for several yards and I could feel it still tugging at my shoulder straps. I was relieved when several dark figures loomed up. At least the chute would be released to stop the tugging. I had no idea of the nature or the extent of my wounds but five minutes later, lying on my back on a wooden table in a small wooden hut lit by one feeble bulb, I had an opportunity to take stock. I figured that I had been shot in the chest because the German soldier who had hoisted me on his back to carry me to the hut had brushed blood onto his hand as he removed my flying jacket. I thought it was a lung because blood was coming from my chest and I found it rather difficult to breathe. Then I caught sight of my arm. I could not make out the details of the wound but saw a bloody, confused, dirty tangle of skin and leather. It did not look too good, I thought, but probably it didn't matter if I had been shot in the lung anyhow.

My breathing was becoming more laboured. It was as if someone was slowly but surely restricting my lung capacity. I had a terrific thirst. I mused for a while, heedless of the whispered instructions being issued around me. I seemed to remember from first aid learned in the past that if internal injury was suspected the patient should not be given anything to drink, but as I was beginning to think my hours were numbered I felt that if I were going to die I would rather do so without a thirst. I called for a drink and took two greedy cups full. It was not water but coffee and it tasted good to me although it was ersatz (make-believe).

As I lay on the table no doubt looking far worse than I really felt (in truth my wounds although messy were numb for the most part and not painful), Dave was brought in, questioned, detained for a while, then bustled out again. Normally of cheery disposition he was unhurt but shaken and no doubt in shock. He told me later that the only thing I said to him at that time was, 'Look what the bastards have done to my new shirt.' The sleeve of my new Van Heusen shirt was torn into shreds. I had just bought it that morning to wear to the dance in King's Lynn that night. I resolved never again to volunteer.

Apart from the mess of my left arm, my leather flying suit was torn above the left knee and along the left thigh. Here again was a mix of blood and leather. The spectacle must have been an unnerving one for onlookers and no doubt Dave was quite sure that he was in the presence of imminent death. Bernie was there too. He had been there before I was brought in and had not spoken a word. He stared in front of him and acted as though he was in a trance. He left with Dave.

Shortly afterwards began what was for me an uncomfortable and seemingly interminable journey by ambulance to a nearby hospital for French POWs. Much of that ride has slipped into the dim mists of the past from which only the most vivid of memories can be drawn, but a few incidents still stand out boldly. I lay on the ambulance stretcher in pain. Yes, it was pain now as the numbness had worn off. It seemed to me, in later months, that the type of pain I experienced then could not be compared with anything I had felt before or since. It seemed mental more than physical. My breath was now coming in short, very short, gasps. I was sure I had not very much longer to live.

I decided that the thing to do was to offer up a prayer before I left this world. I had never been a great churchgoer and I discovered that when I attempted to say the Lord's Prayer there were some lines that I could simply not remember. However, I finished it as best I could and then, tortured by the peculiar type of pain I was experiencing and not being able to see any advantage from dragging it on, I tried to end my life by the simple expedient of holding my breath. It didn't strike me at the time that this was impossible. Fortunately, for the completion of this story and sundry other reasons, I was unsuccessful. After the third attempt I gave up.

I was still breathing in short gasps when the ambulance skidded to a halt on the gravel drive outside a large hospital on the Danish border. Dawn was just breaking and there was a briskness in the air as the sun started to peep over the distant hills. I was in no mood to appreciate this, however, as I was hustled to the operating theatre. There I submitted reluctantly to the sickly smelling mask that was gently placed over my face.

CHAPTER 9
HOSPITALISED IN GERMANY, 1941

If, some weeks later, you had visited the hospital in Schleswig, Germany, which bore the name 'Reserve Lazarette II Stalag XA', entered the main door, turned to the left, walked down the corridor past large wards, through a restroom, past the operating theatre until you reached a wooden door on which are the words 'Defense d'entrer' and, ignoring the warning, opened the door, you'd find yourself in a small room in which there were four beds. Only one of them is occupied — by yours truly. Admittedly it is rather hard to recognise me. I am thin, drawn and pale. I had surprised the doctors and myself by living. I had not been wounded in the lungs as I thought. In fact, it was a small shallow wound almost directly over my heart but harmless enough anyhow, even though it produced a fair amount of blood at the time. Nevertheless I was initially given up for dead.

True, I had nearly died — not from my wounds but rather from loss of blood. The tally to support this was seven wounds altogether, on the arm, leg and chest. An incision in the 1eg, two shrapnel splinters in the liver and a six-inch incision in the stomach from the surgeon completed the score and considerably advanced my claims to the favour of mother luck, particularly since the doctors had taken from the small wound in my chest a complete bullet head which was twisted and misshapen. It had obviously ricocheted from somewhere inside the aircraft and was spent by the time it struck me over the heart. It had enough momentum to go through my leather flying jacket and stick its nose a half inch into my flesh. Destined to be a prize exhibit for the rest of my life, it was stolen from me on the boat going home.

Chapter 9

The building had once housed the insane but now served as a hospital for prisoners of war. Its occupants, excluding the German staff, consisted for the most part of Polish and French prisoners. There were also Belgians, Russians, Czechs, Yugoslavs, one Turk and now one Australian. None of the patients or doctors spoke English.

Fourteen hours after I had surrendered to the chloroform mask I regained consciousness. The room was dark; it was night and the 'blackouts' had been drawn to guard against air raids. As my eyes accustomed themselves to the darkness I could discern a form sitting beside me and decided that it must be a male nurse. I was in a large ward and could hear the moaning and restless tossing of those who could not sleep. I was tortured by a terrific thirst. I called out, 'Could I have some water please?

No response. I repeated my request but still no response. It dawned on me that no-one at all spoke English.

So drawing on my schoolboy French: 'M'sieu j'ai besoin d'eau, síl vous plaît?'

At this the nurse said, 'Desole. Pas d'eau pendant deux jours.'

I was frustrated. Two days without water!

When I look back now I realise what a nuisance I must have been during the following two days with my requests for water, which was not allowed me.

My life had hung in the balance, with the odds against me, but with the help of senior French surgeon Professor René Simon, one of Europe's leading pre-war surgeons, and his Polish colleague, Dr Riskosky, I pulled through. The danger period soon passed and after a week I had recovered sufficiently to be moved from the dressing station to a smaller room. This was managed with some difficulty as both my left arm and left leg were in splints.

I was now alone and while I had no opportunity of speaking English I could converse in French with those who attended and visited me. I had fortunately studied French at school so it was not long before I felt at home in that language and began to read some French books and newspapers that were lent to me. This way I gradually pieced together the missing parts of my puzzle and for the first time began to form a reasonably accurate picture of what had taken place and where I was.

One morning the professor walked in. 'They brought you here early one morning,' he said in French.

'Nous avons pense que vous étiez parti mais vous avez une très forte constitution.' (We thought you were gone but you have a very strong constitution.)

'Vous êtes mal blessé. Lorsque vous avez récupéré vous pouvez être renvoyé.' (You are badly wounded. When you have recovered you may be sent home.)

After some further conversation he departed leaving me with a tantalising thought of possible repatriation, which in the following years gradually faded.

There were several intriguing aspects of my adventure which did not add up. For instance, I knew I was facing the night fighter when he fired and yet I had two bullet holes in my buttocks. Apart from that, the holes which were obviously made by bullets went straight into my flesh for two and three inches respectively and yet there were no bullets at the end of the holes. And no matter how hard I searched, I could not find a single hole or tear in either my trousers or underclothes. My leather flying trousers were tucked into my leather flying boots so I have never been able to understand how the wounds were made when there was no apparent point of entry for the bullets and, indeed, the bullets themselves had disappeared! It was quite a while before I ceased trying to figure out what had really happened.

I came to know and respect the French and Polish doctors, always dressed in white, who visited me. Professor Simon, advancing in age, was of florid complexion, somewhat serious and rather distant in manner. Riskosky was Polish, much younger than Simon, bald-headed, tall and well built, and always smiling.

The various doctors who used to visit me brought with them small gifts which alleviated my lot and one doctor in particular produced a few English books which proved to be a godsend as the hours dragged heavily, with no other Englishmen to speak to. I was also, with the aid of my French, beginning to learn German. This came fairly easily and it was not long before I was reading the national newspapers and magazines.

Things went on this way until the morning of 3 June when Dr Riskosky poked his head around the door and said, 'Bonnes nouvelles. Un autre aviateur Anglais et pour bientot.' (Good news. Another English airman is arriving soon.)

I was so excited. At last someone to speak to and to share news with. Sure enough, he limped in an hour or so later, carrying his yellow Mae West and his flying boots. He had been shot down in Denmark while attacking a ship in a narrow fjord. He was not, however, badly wounded and had merely come to Schleswig for an X-ray. He stayed two days. By this time a Polish Army captain had moved in too so there were now four of us, the remaining bed being occupied by a Belgian soldier whose main claim to fame, it appeared, was that he had played his clarinet before King Leopold.

He and his two French orderly pals took great delight in exchanging obscenities. The Belgian's stay was doomed to be short, however, as on 7 June he was bustled out to make way for another Englishman who was to arrive that day.

At 11.30 am a stretcher was carried in and a tall, skinny figure sporting a large ragged moustache flopped feebly into the vacant bed. It was not until he lay back on his pillow and spoke a few words that I recognised Bill Legg, my observer. I let out a great yell: 'Bill, you bloody beaut!', which startled both Bill and the doctors, not so much because of its volume as from the fact that hitherto I had spoken with very little interest or gusto to anyone. He could not sit up or see me but recognised my voice immediately and, amid a hectic exchange of greetings, I managed to explain to Professor Simon that we were in the same crew. They soon left us to ourselves with strict orders to cut down on the talking. Both of us had thought the other was dead. Through that afternoon, which I shall always remember, we talked, exchanged tales and laughed until the tears ran down our cheeks, an indulgence we regretted later because of the severe pains we inflicted on our weak stomachs.

This is his story as Bill told it.

When Dave reported his turret on fire I grabbed the nearest extinguisher and ran down to the rear to see how I could help. Well, we got the fire under control and I was picking my way back past you in the astro-hatch when something hit me in the back and I fell forward. I saw you lying on your back. I lost consciousness and when I regained my senses I saw you and Dave bailing out at the rear escape hatch. Then I don't remember any more for a bit so I suppose I must have passed out again. When I regained consciousness for the second time you had gone and the interior of the aircraft was empty although it was still flying straight and level so I went forward, clambering with difficulty over the main spar to speak to the pilot.

Imagine, then, my surprise to find that there was no-one at the controls and that the plane was flying by itself. A fierce fire was raging, owing to a stray bullet having set off one of the flares, so I thought I should lose no time in bailing out. That was all very well but I had a dizzy spell when standing by the escape hatch and instead of clipping my parachute onto my chest I dropped it through the hatch and it vanished into the night. There went my only means of saving my life.

And yet several minutes later I was being lifted out of the aircraft, again unconscious, by some German soldiers. I had clambered into the pilot's bucket seat with the intention of diving the aircraft straight into the deck to get it over quickly. But after playing around with the controls and the throttles and finding that everything seemed to work, I decided to postpone the evil moment and fly a while before putting the aircraft into a dive. Then, the urge to self-preservation being as strong as it is, I decided I would try to land the aircraft.

The moon provided some minimal lighting and I could make out a small field crossed with innumerable dykes and surrounded by high tension cables. I figured it was now or never. After bumping down successfully in a wheels-up landing I skidded to a screeching halt, whereupon I lost consciousness once more. German soldiers at the scene extinguished the fire and pulled me from the cabin. Fortunately there was a hospital not more than a few hundred yards away, to which I was rushed. A German doctor operated immediately and I have spent the last month convalescing. I found that I had been shot through the intestines twice, probably by the same burst that got you. I also received shrapnel in the arms and legs, although not serious and I considered myself to be the luckiest man alive until I heard your story.

Chapter 9

So ended his amazing tale and now we knew what had happened to us both. At this point we assumed that the rest of the crew were safe. Subsequently we learned that Andy, the pilot, had been killed and Dave, Bernie and Geoff taken prisoner. Both of us were later listed for repatriation on an injured prisoner exchange scheme. For me it did not happen but for Bill it eventually did, but more of that later.

CHAPTER 10
CONVALESCENCE, 1941

On 13 June 1941, Norm Harris, a wireless operator/air gunner (Wop/AG) who had arrived two days before, left for Frankfurt and a prison camp. His leg had been X-rayed at a nearby German hospital and no bullet could be seen so he was discharged from our hospital quickly. That left a vacancy in our room which was not filled for a few days.

By way of a change we were presented with a Yugoslav private, Jordan, as an orderly. He was a mild man with rough and halting French, willing to do our bidding and beyond. He sometimes risked severe punishment if discovered pilfering the German officers' rations. Apart from a few preliminary differences of opinion we got on quite well with him and it was not long before we had him cooking appetising food, some of it stolen from the German officers' mess and some of it generously contributed to the common fund by the Polish captain who had, it appeared, a loving brother somewhere in Turkey. As a means of passing the time we had taken to teaching the captain to speak English. It was a halting and somewhat boring exercise with Polish words thrown in to the mix. I learned to greet the captain in the morning with 'dzien dobry' (good morning), to call out 'dobre mieko' (good milk), and to congratulate the captain or Jordan with 'bardzo dobre jedzenie (really good food) when they produced an especially tasty dish.

Around this time we were locked in our room continuously. Anyone who wished to see us had to obtain permission to do so. That was, we figured, the reason for giving us an orderly.

I found out that the German officers had noted an increase in morale amongst the French prisoners and had put it down to the tales of British and French advances and the promise that the war would end shortly with an Allied victory, which I was dispensing daily to the groups of French prisoners who used to visit me and stand around my bed.

Chapter 10

We were still compelled to lie flat on our backs, completely immobilised, and our day mostly consisted of reading, talking to the French prisoners and counting the hours to our mealtime. I was handicapped by not being able to write, something which would have helped endure those weary days. I could not straighten my leg, move my back or raise my head, and neither Bill nor I had much sleep for a full month. At night we would lie awake talking, listening to the dull drone of British bombers overhead, tossing fitfully or sipping lukewarm water from a thick glass.

Jordan, the Yugoslav, was forced to vacate his bed on the morning of the 26th when a breathless Polish orderly heralded the arrival of yet another sergeant — this time a pilot. He was badly burnt and the rest of his crew had been killed when a night fighter attacked them. His face was swathed in bandages and the only break in the white mass was a small slit through which he was able to eat and drink. The days dragged slowly through the summer but Peter gradually improved. Soon he could sit up and talk to us and each day he was taken away for attention. He would return each time with fewer bandages than before.

My wounds, too, were visibly improving. I now weighed slightly less than eight stone but was gradually beginning to put on weight. Each two days I received some kind of injection for my liver, which had shrapnel in it. On three occasions I developed a strong fever. I shook so severely on one occasion that the bed squeaked and groaned and the medical record sheet holder on the end bolster rattled loudly for some hours. Because I came from Australia (the other side of the world and therefore mysterious and unknown) the doctors thought it was malaria but a blood test soon disproved this assumption. The fevers, however, were only minor setbacks due to excessive inflammation of my wounds and did nothing to seriously retard my progress.

I had been waiting patiently for my temperature to drop to an acceptable level. For some months now my fever had been worrying the doctors. Eventually one morning Dr Riskosky noticed a drop in my temperature and expressed optimism that things were on the improve. With a smile he said, 'M'sieur, Alex. Lorsque le température descend en dessous de 39 degres, nous allons vous permettre dáller dans le soleil avec votre ami.' (When your temperature drops to below 39 degrees we will allow you to go out into the sun with your friend.)

I finally dragged the temperature down to the magical level and thereafter we spent a few pleasant days lying together in the sun on our stretchers in the green courtyard. It was a very short-lived joy, however, because this year the sun seemed reluctant to put in an appearance and even when it did it possessed no sting. Pete, the sergeant pilot, at this stage had not recovered sufficiently to join us so he had to remain indoors.

By this time I had managed to get an exercise book so I took to keeping a diary and writing short stories, which helped to pass the time. We had also been sending letters home regularly but had received no replies and were giving up hope when on 4 August, after 12 weeks, Bill received his first three letters. Great was the rejoicing as at last we had established a line of communication with home and they knew we were at least alive.

I was now able to hobble around the wards and because of my rapidly improving French I was designated by Professor Simon to be receptionist and interpreter for all new British arrivals. Sometimes badly injured and mutilated airmen were brought in on stretchers and it was my job to obtain from them their name, number and rank before they went under the knife. Sometimes they did not regain consciousness. It was not a pleasant job. And it was growing daily.

To add to the slowly growing tally of English fliers two more arrived on the morning of 9 August and were placed in an adjoining room. Ginger, a Wop/Ag, had sustained a fractured skull and abrasions and John Graham, his pilot, had a broken ankle and a probable broken leg (this was confirmed later). Their plane had crashed at 200 miles per hour, killing one of the crew members. The fourth had been taken straight to Dulag Luft, the German POW reception camp near Frankfurt, having nothing more serious than a few cuts and bruises. They had been shot at by both light and heavy flak and we later had a visit from both an army and a naval officer to determine, if possible, which battery could claim the victory. For the first five or six days Ginger was in a critical condition, but to our relief he recovered quickly due to the good work of Professor Simon and Dr Riskoski. John Graham was moved to our room where on occasions we began to while away the time playing cards.

We had received word that we were to be moved en masse to another hospital in a town called Rendsburg. We had many farewells on that last day at Schleswig and I, who had found my legs, joined in a party that evening with our Polish comrades in their rooms. I was under strong pressure to provide some sort of an act to represent the British airmen and I finally decided to translate a popular English song of the moment, 'Music Maestro Please', into French. It was received with great acclamation.

There were many faces that I saw for the last time that night. Florian Walszack, a Polish medical orderly who had dressed our bandages and attended to us for months, was being sent to a stalag. Countless times we'd heard the key rattle in our door late at night to admit Florian, who served in the German officers' mess. He would have a tidbit of food that he had stolen from the mess. It might be a plate of delightful baby potatoes or a bowl of mouth-watering strawberries or a dish of grilled fish or a lovely dessert, all delicacies that the officers had left over from their evening meal. To do this he had to wait until the German officers were all in their shirt sleeves, having hung their jackets on pegs in an annexe, replete with good French wine, and then he would slip the medical officer's key from his jacket pocket and let himself into our room after stealing whatever was available that night. Then he would wait until we had bolted down his offering and then hurry to return the key to its rightful place. For weeks he risked his life to make life a little more pleasant for us.

Bolic, the brawny cook with the perpetual smile nearly broke the bones in my hands when he said goodbye. There were also the cheery Polish doctors who were bound for a prison camp in Hamburg.

Six o'clock on Saturday morning, 23 August, found us up and dressed, munching some French chocolate we had been given prior to leaving. Together with French and Polish wounded we arrived at Rendsburg after a short though tiring journey by train. The treatment at our new hospital was very good and we were surprised by the friendliness of the French and Belgian prisoners, who gave us chocolate, tobacco and other luxuries. Up to this time we had formed a very poor opinion of most of the French, but those we met at Rendsburg did much to erase our first impressions. The Germans at Rendsburg were much better too and Bill and I were given as much freedom as the other prisoners, a courtesy which had been denied us during the past month by the commandant at Schleswig.

On Thursday 28 August an Irish sailor arrived for observation. There was no mistaking his broad accent. He had been a prisoner since the assault on Navik where he had been badly affected by a bomb blast. He was plainly not in his right senses and was finally despatched to a Hamburg mental hospital for observation, but not before he had given me a German–English dictionary and a sewing set which later proved very useful. 'Thanks, mate,' I said as I bade him farewell, 'I can really make use of these. Good luck.'

Professor Simon and a Polish doctor arrived from our previous hospital on 1 September and needless to say we were glad to see them and to have them continue to attend to us. All my wounds were now healed except for my chest, which was still giving trouble, along with a stabbing pain I felt in my right side. My left arm was being massaged daily in an endeavour to straighten it but no definite improvement was noted. Bill's stomach wound was still in the same condition, and his bowels were discharging regularly from his back because his wound had broken open again.

A Wop/Ag from the Fleet Air Arm was brought in by stretcher on 5 September and after a preliminary inspection was placed in the same ward as the rest of us. This now brought our number to five. Geoff Griffins, the newcomer, had been shot down at Kirkeness some six weeks previously and since then had been leading a very enjoyable life in a Norwegian hospital. His wounds had not seemed to interfere in the least with his lovemaking capacities and the stories of his numerous escapades with some of the willing Norwegian nurses kept us amused. Geoff's plane had been hit by flak and engaged by two fighters simultaneously when he was attacking a German destroyer in a small fjord. He had crashed on a small island adjoining the mainland and was picked up almost immediately. The second toe of his left foot had been shot away and the toes on either side of the stump were broken.

Chapter 10

On 12 September a Canadian pilot named Robert Welbourne was brought in following a big raid on the previous night. He was badly smashed about and, although I did not know it at the time I saw him, he had a broken neck. I tried to talk with him, to reassure him, but he was conscious only for short spells and was obviously, to me anyhow, dying. One foot was hanging by a piece of skin from a bloody leg stump and his whole body was pitted with wounds and bad abrasions. His face, especially the mouth, was horribly mutilated. He had crashed with his plane and had been left in the wreckage for eight hours. I tried to ascertain his service particulars: 'Hi, mate. My name's Alex. What's yours?'

A gurgle answered me.

'I see you're a Canadian. I'm an Aussie but I trained in your country. Can you tell me your number?'

Another gurgle.

He was having great difficulty trying to talk so I resorted to rifling through his pockets to get his name tag, which had his name and number engraved on it. I never exchanged words with him again. He was moved to another hospital but died that night at eight o'clock. Graham and I were present at the funeral three days later when a company of Luftwaffe troops fired a salute of three volleys over the grave. A beautiful wreath was presented by the prisoners at Rendsburg and another was provided by the Luftwaffe. We regretted most that we could not contribute a single German mark towards the cost because we had no money.

On the morning after the funeral yet another pilot was brought in, but we were relieved to find he was not badly wounded. He turned out to be a Kiwi, Bob Blakeway, hailing from Christchurch. Three members of his crew were killed and two were still at large. I discovered that the dead captain was a pilot I had trained with in Scotland as was proven by two charred identity discs which were brought in by a German Army officer. A burst of heavy flak had blown a hole in both sides of the aircraft and Bob, the survivor who was standing between the two holes, had sustained innumerable splinter wounds in the arms and legs.

About this time we were examined by a medical board consisting of two German doctors, the professor and a Polish doctor. Afterwards the professor came to our room and said 'You are going home, to England.' This was the first of several repatriation schemes and was introduced towards the end of 1941. We had previously heard that 1000 wounded prisoners were to be exchanged between Germany and Great Britain and it now seemed that we would be among the lucky ones. We were to go first to Wiesbaden and then to Calais. We were elated, naturally, but our joy was short-lived; the exchange never took place. Instead we were sent to prison.

CHAPTER 11
OFF TO PRISON CAMP, 1941

Two days later, after many farewells, I left Rendsburg. With me were Ginger and Graham. The others were to follow at a later date when an ambulance train could be procured. At eight o'clock on a nippy morning we boarded a train bound for Hamburg on the first stage of our journey, escorted by two armed soldiers who could speak English. Train services were disrupted as might be expected given the constant bombing of rail links throughout Germany. Following a wait of three hours in a Hamburg restaurant, where we were happy to find a seat and have a rest, we caught another train for Hanover and after much changing of trains we staggered into the Hanover station at seven o'clock in the evening, dog-tired. In a nearby cafe we sat down to some Red Cross soup, the focus of many curious eyes. At all the stops we had on our journey the Red Cross ladies were always courteous and helpful, and generous with their ladles of steaming vegetable soup.

As we were sipping our soup the public address system suddenly blared out in deafening tones: 'Achtung! Achtung! Das Oberkommando des Heeres verkunden die tapferen truppen uberwaltigt Kiev und genommen tausende von gefangenen. Heil Hitler!' (Attention! Attention! The High Command of the Army announces that the brave troops of our army have overwhelmed Kiev and taken thousands of prisoners. Heil Hitler!)

This announcement was met with loud cheers from the German patrons. The offensive of the German Army in Russia was gaining momentum and their troops were headed menacingly towards Moscow, killing thousands of Russian soldiers and taking millions of prisoners as they went. The Russians were laying waste to their countryside as they retreated and were inflicting losses on the German armies which became crippling as the cold winter progressed. It was not long after that that the pace of the German advance began to slow. Months later the merciless winter set in in earnest and the Germans bogged down within sight of their main objective — Moscow. Unable to move in the snow and ice and without food and warmth, thousands froze to death. Two years later, under far more optimistic circumstances, we were to hear of the recapture of Kiev by the conquering Russian armies.

We returned from the café to the station in the blackout and boarded the 8.52 for Kassel. After being thwarted there in an attempt to take the fast train, we spent the remainder of a cold night sleeping in a stationary carriage in Hanover from which we were dragged at 5 am to continue our journey south. By now we were feeling rather sick; this was the first time we had been on our feet for more than an hour or so since being shot down, and after another long wait at Bad Hamburg we caught the final train for Ober Ursel, where the POW reception camp known as Dulag Luft was located. It was almost noon and the sun was shining brightly down on the gleaming rails when we completed our journey, during which we had changed trains eight times.

We were greeted in a small waiting room by a Luftwaffe Feldwebel (sergeant) who spoke good English and who had a fine car waiting for us. A Canadian airman was also being detained in the waiting room. He had evaded capture after descending by parachute, until lack of food and lack of knowledge of the country had forced him to give himself up. He turned out to be one of the two members of Bob Blakeway's crew, who were at large when Bob (the Kiwi) was carried into our ward at Rendsburg.

Dulag Luft (Durchgang Lager — transit camp) was a pleasant camp, though the reason for that was obvious enough. They wanted information from us. It was here that all airmen were interrogated, by way of a Red Cross form of very doubtful authenticity, after a good meal. At this period of the war, Dulag Luft was the receiving centre for all captured air force personnel and from there they were despatched to the various stalags (for NCOs) and oflags (for officers).

Chapter 11

The interview was conducted as a one-on-one by a young Luftwaffe officer who was quite friendly and pleasant. The questions were innocuous enough at the start, asking for our name, number and rank. After that came personal details such as religion, nationality, next of kin, place of birth and so on. Then followed questions about squadron, size of crew, length of service, treatment by captors, and so on. The questions were carefully worded to appear harmless and to elicit information that we were expressly told to avoid discussing, but no pressure was exerted on me to answer any questions that I did not want to. I'm sure that most prisoners would have given only what they were obliged to by international law; name, rank and number. The interviewing officer spoke flawless English and maintained a polite demeanour throughout although he was obviously frustrated at my refusals. Not everyone had the soft treatment like me. Perhaps it was because I had taken so long to get to the transit camp that all my answers would have been out of date.

After interrogation, as a result of my constant complaining that we were not yet fully recovered, we were again placed in a car and whisked up the road to a small hospital in a glade at the edge of a great pine forest. It was a beautiful setting and we were in no way disappointed when we entered, as we found many other Commonwealth fliers already there. For the past 12 hours I had had a recurrence of the sharp pains in the region of my liver each time I took a deep breath, so I was immediately put to bed and in two days the pain had disappeared. The food we received from then onwards was a jolly sight better than that we had been given in North Germany, and the prisoners' ward of the hospital had a large library and many games. That night, undisturbed by air raid sirens, I enjoyed my slumbers with the comfort of a soft, down pillow, the first I had enjoyed since becoming a prisoner.

Life in Dulag hospital was a welcome change from our previous existence. We were given a breakfast consisting of bread rolls and jam with coffee, which we took in the small ante-room used as a dining room. We could then spend the mornings on a small open balcony, lying in the sun, reading and smoking English cigarettes, of which we received a plentiful supply. Lunch was a plate of good soup followed by a course of potatoes and vegetables, all topped off with a dessert course such as ice-cream or fruit compote. Tea and cakes would be brought in at 3 pm, providing an afternoon break, and for the evening meal we would have bread rolls and perhaps salad, followed by English tea. 'Lights out' was at 9 pm after a game of Monopoly or cards and we would snuggle into comfortable beds in rooms of four beds.

On Saturday 27 September, 15 men left for other hospitals as part of a plan to vacate the Dulag hospital and shortly after that Bill arrived from Rendsburg. He told me that the four of them (one more had arrived since my departure) had come down from the lazarette (hospital) on an ordinary train. It had proved a better journey than ours, by all accounts, although Bill had fainted during the second day. He was really in no fit condition to travel, his back being no better than it was when I had seen him last.

On 30 September at 8 o'clock in the morning, seven more departed, depleting our numbers considerably. By 4 o'clock on the same afternoon, we too were on our way to a destination unknown. Our processing was complete and we were now being transferred to a regular prison camp. Bill had remained, presumably to undergo another operation. The repatriation, it appeared, was now definitely off so we had not even seen Wiesbaden or Calais from a distance. We were getting used to false alarms when it came to repatriation so although the news originally excited me I accepted the cancellation somewhat stoically and turned my attention to the immediate future. I was under the impression that we were bound for yet another hospital as my wound had not yet healed but to my surprise we found ourselves in a dismal gaol used for French prisoners in the old town of Mainz.

Mainz was renowned for being the birthplace of Gutenberg whose invention of the printing press was second only to that of the wheel for revolutionising human society. In 1445 he transformed life and initiated the Renaissance with his communication device and from then on ignorance slowly declined and the Church began to lose its stranglehold on knowledge.

The day after we became incarcerated in a dungeon in Mainz, Wing-Commander Douglas Bader, the legless English fighter ace, joined us and told us his story.

'I was leading 17 Squadron when our Hurricanes were attacked by a flight of Messerschmit 109s. It was a free-for-all and in the process I was shot down. As I was going down I found that I could not get my leg free. Fortunately my Hurricane was not on fire. I fought and pulled and tried to twist my foot sideways but I could not free it. I was getting too close to the ground for comfort. I was sweating and counting the seconds as I lost height. Finally, with a flash of desperation I thought to unstrap my metal leg and leave it in the plane. I inverted the aircraft and bailed out with one leg left. Fortunately I still had enough height to open my chute and land safely.'

We listened, fascinated, as he told us of his reception by the Luftwaffe who subsequently arranged for a temporary truce in order to allow a RAF transport aircraft to fly to Germany to drop a spare leg to the Wing Commander. It was in a large well-padded box.

It was this box, heavy as it was with all his kit, which we had to carry around for days as we were moved from Mainz up north to Lubeck. My path crossed his several times at different prison camps. The last time I saw him was in 1947 when he visited Perth as a PR representative working for the Shell Oil Company.

Conditions in the prison at Mainz were abominable. We were confined in an underground dungeon which was dank and dark. The forbidding granite walls oozed dampness in what was to me a classic *Prisoner of Zenda* setting. It was quite depressing to say the least. The food was repulsive and our spoons and forks were dirty. After vehement protests by W/C Bader we were moved two days later to a camp at Lubeck. Before the war — in the early 1930s — the pilots of different air forces used to meet on occasions for flying demonstrations and contests and it was at these meetings that Bader met several young German pilots. They formed friendships and retained communication with one another for a while after the flying meetings ceased as war approached. With the passage of time many of his pre-war friends had now become generals in the Luftwaffe. It was fortunate for us because he demanded that his complaint be forwarded to one of these officers.

There were seven of us: four sergeants and three officers. The first day's travelling terminated at a small station en route, where we were given a hot meal and a bed by the Red Cross, who were very good to us at all stops. We were quite surprised because we fully expected to get only basic treatment from the Red Cross orderlies as we were obviously prisoners and equally obviously airmen, who were not very popular in that area of Germany. As usual our train journey was a matter of stops and starts because damage had been done to the major lines throughout western Germany by the night bomber raids. At five o'clock on a bitterly cold morning we set off again, heading north, and travelled all through that day and evening, stopping only to change trains and gulp down a quick meal of Red Cross soup.

On the night of the second day, at 9.30 pm, we stumbled onto the platform at Lubeck, glad to see the end of an exhausting journey. Lubeck was an oflag (officers camp), and therefore not the final destination for the sergeants among us, as we had believed. For the officers it certainly was the end, but for us it was merely the beginning of another, though much shorter, journey. We were turned back (so near and yet so far), whisked to a train once more and taken back to Hamburg from where we commenced a five-hour ride to Berlin. After much more changing in Berlin tube stations at six o'clock in the morning, where we met bleary-eyed workmen returning from a night of toil mingling with bright-eyed clerks fresh from their morning wash, we finally caught a southbound train and found ourselves on the last stage of our travels, 40 miles south of Berlin.

At 10 o'clock on the morning of Saturday 4 October I was taken through the gates of Stalag IIIE, weary, bleary and thoroughly fed up with travelling, the novelty having long since worn off.

CHAPTER 12
STALAG IIIE: KIRCHAIN, GERMANY, 1941

An uncertain sun was shining down on the fallen autumn leaves and dusty paths leading to Stalag IIIE. Its beams peered through a patched sky, but although a noticeable crispness could be felt in the air, aided by a playful breeze, one would not have thought it to be October weather. Groups of prisoners could be seen scattered here and there on blankets laid on the grassy courtyard of the wired-in compound. The whole camp, small though it was, looked attractive and comfortable from a distance, but when we approached we could see the lack of living room and cooking facilities, and the crude sanitary arrangements.

Until that moment my life since being shot down had been varied — pain and pleasure, highs and lows, surprises and disappointment — but never in my time as a prisoner so far had I had to confront the reality of being held against my will by armed guards. I saw barbed wire close up for the first time and realised its grim purpose. I was uncomfortable with the German soldiers in army uniform with their rifles slung over their shoulders. I realised with a jolt that life would be vastly different from now on from the gentle and friendly attitude of the hospital staff and doctors and the French prisoners. It dawned on me that I was now a real prisoner. Home seemed much further away than it did before I had to enter those wooden barbed wire gates. Gone was the dream of repatriation. Now I was just a number (182). There was also so much to find out about our new gaolers. So it was with some trepidation that I walked through the gates and joined the prisoners behind the wire.

The prisoner strength was 184 Allied aircrew and the first task for new arrivals that day was to find accommodation in one of the four huts the camp comprised. I eventually settled in the largest one with 65 others. Though we had three-tier wooden beds and many were sleeping two in a bed (for warmth), I was fortunate to secure a top bunk for myself. I did not have much in the way of personal belongings so it did not take long to get my little space organised. On arrival we had to surrender our boots and were issued with wooden clogs, presumably to make it more difficult to escape. They were very cumbersome and uncomfortable and certainly prevented the wearer from running any distance. These remained on the floor.

After lunch I began a tour of the other huts to see if any of my friends had preceded me to the camp. I found five English airmen from my operational training unit at Lossiemouth but saw no-one else I knew, whereas Taffy, Ginger and Bill, my travelling companions from the hospital, having been completely trained in England over a period of months, came across many former English friends. Of the 184 prisoners only four were Australian. That was not surprising as the arrival of Australian aircrews both in England and the Middle East was just starting to bear fruit.

I soon discovered that our food ration was so sparse that we had to learn to accustom ourselves to being in a constant state of hunger. I realised that by comparison we had fared rather well in hospital. In camp we were issued with one-eighth of a loaf of black bread per person per day. A small cube of margarine and a spoonful of ersartz jam were accompanied by a bowl of soup which usually had small pieces of dried fish or potatoes or swede turnips floating in it. Sometimes it had pieces of meat floating in it. In the mornings we were issued with jugs of hot ersatz tea. Many of the prisoners spurned the tea and others used it to shave with.

The camp had a small library but it was hopelessly inadequate and I found that many of the fellows were busily engaged in unusual activities to pass the time. For instance, some were making small dark cakes from their bread crusts, which were tasty and soft. The cakes themselves, after they were baked in a crude oven made of tins, tasted quite rich, though they were very heavy and often proved too much for the prisoners' weak stomachs. They also required you to save bread crusts instead of eating them, which needed quite an act of willpower. In these conditions the habits and actions of some of the prisoners would have been hard for a well-fed person to understand.

Not many days after my arrival, a representative of the American Embassy paid the camp a visit and on hearing that the boys had not received a single Red Cross parcel, promised a batch within a month or so. The spirits of the whole camp rose perceptibly; many of the prisoners, particularly the younger ones who had never been far from home, were beginning to let the deprivation of freedom get them down. In addition to relieving the food problem, the Red Cross parcels would provide us with cigarettes, thereby removing a constant source of concern. The shortage of cigarettes had become so acute that men were saving their cigarette butts and rolling cigarettes in small scraps of newspaper.

From this you can probably imagine, then, the reception accorded Ginger when he poked his mop of red hair through the doorway of No. 1 Hut and announced excitedly the arrival at the gate of a wagon loaded to the brim with Red Cross parcels.

'Hey! Chaps! There's a wagon full of Red Cross parcels at the gate!'

'Ar get lost, Ginger. That'll be the day. The Yank said three or four weeks and it's only been two. You're a bloody rumour-monger, Ginger.'

'Okay. Come and see for yourselves,' retorted Ginger. 'They look like the real thing from here.'

And sure enough they were.

Most of the fellows favoured him with a stony disbelieving glare, while some of them muttered 'more rumours' and others were less polite. A shallow laugh floated across the room from a red-bearded sergeant lying on his top bunk. It was Tiny, the hut pessimist (there always has to be one in every hut), who turned back to his book and lost himself in misery once more. 'All right, see for yourself,' retorted Ginger, in no way daunted, and pointed with a freckled finger.

Sure enough, the wagon had entered the compound and nestling on the boards, side by side, could be seen many small cardboard boxes bearing the familiar Red Cross on their lids. Seeing was believing. Ginger retired, triumphant but unnoticed, and within a minute plans were underway for a great feast that night. At this stage, Tiny poked his pessimistic nose over the leaves of his book and said, 'The parcels are just as likely to contain clothing as food!' This dampened the boys' spirits for a minute until news came back that they definitely were food parcels, 440 in all, and plans went on afresh.

No.1 Hut that night was transformed beyond recognition. Small groups of men were scattered here and there comparing possessions, and the aroma of herrings, bacon, Irish stew, pineapples, cocoa and many other foodstuffs, the smell and taste of which we had almost forgotten, permeated the atmosphere.

'Hey, Alex!' said Freddie Woods, 'This honey tastes a lot better than the honey we used to get at home.'

'That's because it's Australian,' I said with a grin.

'Bloody Aussies,' retorted Freddie. 'Always exaggerating. I bet our Scotch porridge can't be beaten in the land down under. And what about our Yorkshire pudding and our kippers for breakfast?'

I had to capitulate and we concentrated on enjoying the first delicacies we had had in months.

It took many of us back to those days of our youth when, on Christmas Day, we would rush eagerly next door to compare contents of stockings with a pal. Those who had begun to let prison life get them down were now whistling and singing without a care or worry except whether, for instance, they had put too much water in the porridge they were making.

Even the pessimist was squatting cross-legged on his bed stowing away a tin of pork sausages with a dazed 'too good to be true' expression on his face. Coincidentally, with the arrival of food and cigarettes came an issue of underclothing and overcoats, plus another blanket, so the nights became less forbidding as we were greeted with the prospects of a reasonably warm sleep.

Prisoners tended to group together in small numbers to share whatever belongings they had — these groups were called combines. Freddie, my combine partner, fell victim to a run of dysentery in the camp. So he took his blankets and belongings with him and emigrated to No. 4 Hut, which had been converted into a temporary sick bay, there to stay for many months.

On 24 October a general camp meeting was called in No. 1 Hut to discuss the situation regarding the issue of Red Cross parcels, which had ceased after each man had received two parcels. The German authorities always opened the tins in the parcels on delivery. So we prisoners could accept the whole parcel — jam, fish, milk, meats, biscuits, etc. — emptied into one billy can in an awful glutinous sloppy mess, which the Germans were insisting on doing, or refuse to accept the parcels altogether, on principle. This would be a hard decision to make after we had tasted the goodies contained in the parcels.

After more than an hour of debate, during which several different policies were argued for, a vote was taken. I was for refusing on principle and procrastinating, knowing that the International Red Cross representatives would raise the matter with the German authorities as soon as they got word of the commandant's action, which was contrary to the Geneva Convention on the treatment of war prisoners. Fortunately refusal won the day. The commandant, whose bluff had been called, eventually saved face by offering a solution which was more or less a compromise and the distribution was resumed on 29 October, much to our relief. Each man received two parcels on the same day and as we were due to leave for another stalag on 4 November there was much overeating. We succeeded, despite the short time at our disposal, to consume all the foodstuffs by the evening of Monday 3 November, and prepared ourselves for an eight-hour journey northwards.

The purpose of this journey was none too pleasant, but in no way could it be avoided. In No. 2 Hut evidence of lice was apparent and before they had an opportunity to spread, the commandant, fearing typhoid, had decided to have the whole camp deloused. We packed all our clothes and rations for the journey and handed in our valuables to the camp man of confidence, F/Sgt Bingham, to be deposited with the Germans for safe-keeping until our return.

At 3.30 am on a chilly morning we were roused and paraded (after a hot brew of English tea) outside the hut. The early November snow had temporarily ceased to fall but the ground was white and gleaming beneath the electric lights that shone at regular intervals around the compound. There was very little talking — it was too cold for that — and after a final brief check-up we marched silently off, greatcoats buttoned to the neck, parcels in hand, blankets slung over our shoulders.

As we became warmer through marching, so our spirits rose and soon we were singing those old familiar marching tunes that have lived through thick and thin, born in a war-torn world of 25 years ago and outliving many of their would-be successors. It brought back to my mind the happy, carefree days when, in the militia, I had marched to those songs in the company of many of my friends. At that time we hadn't a care in the world. But for the presence of the green-uniformed guards, with slung rifles, we might well have been a company of those boys returning from manoeuvres in peacetime.

Following a cold and uncomfortable train journey spent in a cattle truck designed for 40 hommes and eight chevaux, we arrived at our destination by midday and then began a strenuous march from the railway station to the camp. It could have been no more than two miles at the most, but in the wooden clogs with which we had been issued it seemed far more. No time was lost upon arrival there. We were herded into a mass delousing room where we stood under several banks of showers dispensing hot water and used lumps of rough soap to rid ourselves of our dangerous pests while our clothes were heated and deloused in an adjoining room. Within two hours we were dressing again, beards gone, heads shaven and feeling clean. After we had been installed in clean barracks we took the opportunity of looking around us.

Luckenwalde was a large camp comprising 40,000 prisoners of all nationalities, including Russians fresh from the Eastern front. It was a working camp; that is, all the prisoners were required to join working parties each day, under German guard, and it possessed a large canteen from which we purchased many things we lacked. Those articles we could not buy (lack of money being a vital problem) we obtained from the Frenchmen in the adjoining barrack by way of exchanging bars of soap and English cigarettes and other items from the Red Cross parcels we had brought with us.

A tall French soldat approached me with a smile and said, 'Bonjour. Souhaiitez-vous un peu de chocolat Belge en échange de quelque cigarettes Anglaises?' (Hello. Would you like some Belgian chocolate in exchange for some English cigarettes?)

'Mais oui!' I replied, 'Laisez moi votre chocolat s'il vous plait.' (Yes. Please let me see your chocolate). 'Je vais vous donner vingt woodbines.' (I will give you 20 Woodbines.)

'Non,' he replied, 'je l'échange pour cinquante.' (I will exchange for 50 cigarettes.)

'Trop,' I said. (That's too much.) 'Je me contenterai pour trente-cinq.' (I will settle for 35.)

The deal was done at 35 and we parted company content with the outcome.

Among other things, I obtained writing materials, paper and pencils, of which I was painfully short. I think I can safely say that every man slept that night, contented from his bargaining, munching French biscuits and reflecting upon the obvious advantage of an outing like this when one was short of supplies and wanted a change of surroundings.

Our stay there soon terminated, however, and in 12 hours we were on our way back, this time elevated to the luxury of third-class carriages. There followed the same long march from the station back to Kirchain, but fortunately the weather was kind and somehow the return march did not seem so onerous. Maybe it was because we were feeling much cleaner than we had felt for some weeks. Needless to say, we were glad to get back to our bunks at the camp and no doubt the commandant was equally glad to have us back without mishap — that is, without an attempted escape. Though strong fumes from the disinfectant gasses still persisted, we soon fell soundly asleep and the next day returned to the usual uneventful routine of stalag life.

CHAPTER 13
SETTLING INTO PRISON LIFE, 1941

Two long-awaited letters arrived on 7 November, one from Aunt Mary in Scotland and the other from my cousin Pat in Australia. The latter had taken seven weeks, which was considered exceptionally fast and can be explained by the fact that it had come by Yankee clipper, via the USA and UK. Another letter, this time from home, followed them on the next day and this put me in a good mood. In the letter from home I heard that my sister had given birth to a baby girl. I also heard that two of my friends had been killed in action since I last had any communication with home.

On 12 November Taffy and I moved from No. 1 Hut to No. 4, which had ceased to function as a hospital. Freddie was there and he and I again formed a combine with our Red Cross parcels and cigarettes; we shared everything we received, even the odd slice of bread. It proved very satisfactory to both of us and a lot of our time was whiled away preparing food and washing dirty pans.

Three days after this a member of the American Embassy visited us and inspected the camp and following close on his heels came a Red Cross representative accompanied by a tall, genial, English-speaking officer of the German Army.

Our camp leader, Bingham, spoke with both the Red Cross representative and the German officer to voice our complaints. They were both fluent in English.

'We can't walk properly in these clogs,' he said, knowing that the Germans had confiscated our boots and issued us with wooden clogs to make escaping more difficult. (Actually, 52 of us did subsequently escape without difficulty, all wearing clogs!)

'And the food is very basic. Our soup consists of a few potatoes and some cabbage floating in a tub of hot water with only occasional signs of any meat or a piece of dried fish. Sometimes turnips and sauerkraut provide a change of diet. We are all losing weight. We could do with some more blankets too — it's getting very cold now. And we could certainly do with some more Red Cross parcels. We rely on them to give us badly needed sustenance and we're needing them more as the cold weather sets in.'

The German officer winced when Bingham described the soup, but he replied without rancour: 'I've made a note of your complaints and I shall do what I can though I can't promise anything. We are all on basic rations and meat is particularly hard to come by.'

'I will try to have some more parcels directed to this camp,' promised the Red Cross representative. 'We can do that but I'm not sure of the date because train schedules have been disrupted by the bombing.'

We thanked them and after a cursory examination of the huts and the ablution facilities they went on their way.

On this same day we were treated to our first bath for some months, an event which, although somewhat tarnished by the conditions accompanying it, was yet sufficient of a novelty to evoke much comment for a day or two. It was necessary for two of us to bathe together, and six men (that is three pairs) were compelled to use the same water owing to the difficulty of obtaining sufficient hot water. This was partly remedied, however, by the installation several days later of a boiler which although somewhat uncertain and temperamental, usually provided enough hot water for one complete hut each day.

On 18 November we received a batch of magazines which were readily accepted by the boys as providing light and entertaining reading to pass away idle moments. They were mostly illustrated magazines depicting the history of Britain and, as can be imagined, after the first fortnight or so it was not uncommon to hear dates, battles, politicians and inventors quoted by those whose interests hitherto probably had lain in different areas.

An expectant air hung around the camp on the afternoon of 1 December. Prisoners who had previously allowed all types of growth to adorn their chins appeared clean shaven, myself included. Clean collars and ties which had lain in neglected seclusion for many months appeared in a surprisingly large number. Prisoners, as well dressed as prisoners can be, strolled around the compound smoking innumerable cigarettes looking pretty for one day. Today was to be almost as important a day in our existence here as that on which our first food parcels arrived. We were to have our photographs taken!

This was permitted by the commandant and we were able to send them home to our families. We were taken out of the compound and lined up in front of the kommandantur, which made our surroundings appear ever so much cleaner and more comfortable than they really were. The canteen funds were sufficient to supply the cost of printing and it was only a matter of a fortnight before the prints were given to us. Every group shot was good and we were delighted with them.

Three days later we all received the first of a series of three typhus inoculations and were vaccinated into the bargain. Very few of us felt the effects, however, and a day was sufficient to dispel the languid feeling and stiffness usually accompanying inoculations. Red Cross blankets, pyjamas and handkerchiefs arrived on 4 December and as there were not enough to go round they were drawn for by cutting a pack of cards. It was a further consignment from the Red Cross and we could not have given that organisation sufficient praise.

I shuddered to consider what our position would be were the Red Cross to forsake us. Had their timely help not arrived when it did I feel sure that a few of the weaker of us would not have survived the rigours of the winter which was to follow. As it was, a spirit of intense optimism and a cheerful sense of humour manifested itself in all our words and actions, due in a major part to the constant supply of food parcels and secondly to the continually improving news we heard, from time to time, regarding the efforts of our forces and their allies. In retrospect 1941 was plainly a bad year for the Allies, but we tended to think of the news selectively.

We had learned to take the bad with the good here, meeting every contingency with an attempt at cheerfulness and a confidence in the conviction that with every day our chances of soon being home improved. Even the most pessimistic could not see the war lasting much beyond 1943, especially if America entered the war.

We commenced to run auctions on the distribution day of Red Cross parcels. The house auction was conducted by Doug Elder, who proved himself capable of running a humorous and sensible show.

Prisoners dropped in from other houses to bid for articles they needed. For example, a packet of porridge when put up for sale might fetch a large tin of syrup or a tin of honey plus 10 cigarettes. In this way the boys satisfied their own tastes, ridding themselves of those foodstuffs which did not appeal to them and acquiring other articles that satisfied their palates.

It was around this time, early December 1941, that Finland, Rumania and Hungary declared war on Great Britain and — more important still — Japan entered the conflict, bringing in the USA and leaving no other great power neutral. It was now just about as complete a world war as could be imagined with only Sweden, Spain and Switzerland as neutrals and it seems impossible that any future struggle can ever assume proportions as great, although no war could exceed the brutality and horror of World War I.

Japan opened her account with the raid on Pearl Harbor, the strong American Pacific base, followed up her initial success with the sinking of the British battleships *Repulse* and *Prince of Wales*, and made a strong drive through Siam towards the Malay Peninsula, a series of victories which threw gloom over our camp. Bing, our camp captain, was dethroned at this time and Jock Alexander, who spoke fluent German, succeeded him with a greater degree of success. He was a level-headed and popular leader with a mop of red hair and a marked Scottish accent.

The festive season was now not far off so we began to decorate our hut with a view to spending as merry a Christmas as possible under the circumstances. Tinsel, silver paper, chocolate wrappings, cardboard and other articles we had contrived to accumulate over a period of one month were produced from their storage place and hung with varying degrees of success from ceiling and walls. The 'boat', a cardboard creation in which we placed all our hopes and around which all talk revolved ('the boat that takes us home') was suspended from the ceiling in the place of honour by the door with a silver-covered cardboard model of a Wellington bomber, accompanied by a silver Hurricane, escorting it. The name of the boat was *Hope* and we all felt that it was not far off. Viewed in retrospect, those hopes that we entertained in Christmas 1941 now seem to have been founded on nothing but blind faith and clearly show the way the mind of a normal prisoner refuses to accept a long-term view of unpleasant incarceration.

On 22 December we were all paraded and marched to the local township where we saw several German travel and educational films in English. The screening lasted about an hour and when we arrived back at the camp, cold and somewhat tired, we were glad to hear that the Red Cross Christmas parcels had arrived, as had the piano we had hired for three days. That night we held our first general knowledge bee, which proved popular enough to be repeated once or twice a week for a long period afterwards. Cigarettes donated by the more affluent members of the hut (non-smokers) served as prizes and I think every man profited from the bee in one way or another.

I had plenty of time to think in prison camp and to reflect on my surroundings. I occasionally expressed my thoughts either in verse or in prose. Three poems survived. Here is the first, born of observations of those around me:

Which One Are You?

There are many and various types to be found
In all walks of life, you'll agree
And numerous characters flaunted abound
While others choose veiled secrecy

There's the gift of command some bring to the fore
The aggressive and dominant set
They lead, others follow, their faith is so sure
All obstacles firmly are met

There's always the optimist, merry and bright
An undaunted spirit within
A cheery 'good morning' — a cheery 'goodnight'
A smile through thick and through thin

There's the chap who conceals in a cloak of reserve
His spirit, inactive, retired
But if it's a question of guts or of nerve
He's always in front, he's admired

There's the eternal grumbler, the man with a grudge
To whom nothing ever looks swell
With him even eating's an adjective drudge
Spud peeling's a positive hell

We've got them all here, and a few more as well
The hoarder, the crawler, the sneak
Without them admittedly life would be dull
Its aspect uncomfortably bleak

So reflect for a while, then read this again
If that is not too much to do
I think you will find here seven types of men
And ask yourself, which one are you?

CHAPTER 14
FIRST CHRISTMAS IN PRISON, 1941

Christmas Eve dawned fine and clear and it seemed that we would have to spend a snowless Christmas, but throughout the day the sky slowly changed. Early in the afternoon snow began to fall, slowly at first then with increasing intensity until the ground was covered with a soft, white mantle and the barbed wire enclosing the compound glistened like a network of silver thread. The guards in their watchtowers stamped their feet and clapped their hands in the cold wind. We did not feel sorry for them.

We all prepared our individual Christmas Eve feasts and then, after a brief wash, made our way across to No. 2 Hut where we found half the camp already assembled. Chairs had been brought from the other huts, beds had been cleared away, and a rude stage had been constructed from table tops. This was our makeshift theatre and tonight was the night of nights. A concert had been arranged, of which the main item was a pantomime, written and produced within the precincts of our stalag.

The entertainment soon got underway and as every item was more or less humorous, even the most morbid of us soon forgot his troubles and worries and entered into the spirit of it with many a laugh and hearty handclap. The pantomime was the tragic story of a prince among prisoners who falls in love with Miss Putten Take, the commandant's daughter, but in doing so incurs the wrath of her father. Fearing trouble, the prince escapes from the prison and hides in the country ignorant of the fact that a few hours later the armistice is signed. He is happily rescued some weeks later when a special search party, including Miss Putten Take, discovers him. The show was received with great applause and took up a major part of the entertainment.

The other items, no less popular, soon came to an end and we gathered around the piano for a sing song. German Corporal Schiller read a message from the commandant, in which he wished us as merry a Christmas as circumstances would allow. Then a brew of English tea was announced and the party broke up. As the lads took their mugs and stood around the piano, singing all our popular songs, the thoughts they conjured up filled me with an overwhelming home-sickness and I stole out into the frosty night for a few minutes by myself.

The flakes had ceased to fall and the ominous snow clouds of the afternoon had gracefully retired in favour of the filmy white formations that scudded silently across the sky. The bright rays of a healthy moon shone fitfully down on the expanse of white beneath, such times as they were not intercepted and dispersed by the playful clouds. The stars twinkled in the crisp night with an unaccustomed brilliance, shining to the earth through an atmosphere that seemed infinite. What could be seen of the sky was not blue; it was almost black, adding even greater lustre to the silky clouds, the blinking stars, and the moon which rode serenely above them all, its beaming face seeming to radiate cheerfulness and good humour to all the world. It was as though all nature's forces had collaborated to blend their finest qualities into their 'night of nights' and the result had exceeded their utmost expectations. The stellar spectacle was oblivious to the mass killing that was going on down on earth.

My gaze fell from the heavens to my immediate surroundings. Electric lights, dotted at regular intervals round the compound, shed their light on the glistening snow beneath them where it was reflected back in a thousand different directions by the sparkling crystals. The snow was dry, and the atmosphere crisp and bracing. A strong chilly wind swept across the compound and round the huts whipping small drifts of snow into light flurries of soft white flakes which leapt, whirling, into the air only to settle on the ground a few feet farther on.

I shivered as the cold wind struck through my clothes, but still the spell of the night held me there. I thought of home, of my family and all of my friends, of all the scenes that the tunes I had just heard had conjured up. My thoughts turned from home to the times I had enjoyed since I left it in 1940 and the fine people I had met who had suddenly disappeared from my life, and I turned into the hut again. Such reflections were unwise in the confines of a prison camp.

The party broke up shortly afterwards and the boys dispersed to their various huts to eat their Christmas feasts. We had a special extension of 'lights out' so we spent our time visiting the other huts at midnight and wishing them all 'Merry Christmas'. On Christmas Day we were again assembled and marched to the nearby town of Kirchain where Norman Hennessy, a fellow prisoner, conducted a service in one of the town's fine churches.

Looking at the black sky night after night and listening to the drone of invading aircraft brought rather unpleasant thoughts of what was happening and of the consequences. They are reflected in a 1942 poem that I wrote.

Dark Shapes
Dark falls the night, a mantle black, upon the land —
a land at war
The birds cease flight and nestle down — their day is o'er
For others, then, the work of death is just begun — exacting work
Untiring men, the task before them to be done — they never shirk.

The dark shapes stand on the landing field now dull — a tribute grim
Swift is the brand of death they carry in their hull —
in lines so slim
Before the night has lifted from their outlines black — they will have killed
Before those dark familiar shapes come winging back — some voice is stilled.

Each night the same, a duty grim but too severe — they carry on
They have no shame at all and neither have they fear —— all feeling gone
Some don't return, for them the bitter fight for life —
is over now
For them we yearn and also know that all this strife must end somehow.

86

Chapter 14

The day will come when those dark shapes will lie at rest — no more to kill
Their deadly hum no longer throbbing from their breast — their engines still
In later years those nights of terror will revive —
in memory
Grim souvenirs of those who flew and gave their lives — to keep us free.

On 29 December while the festive season was still in full swing, my first personal parcel arrived. I was overjoyed as it meant that probably not long would elapse before others followed it. There was a certain mystery surrounding it, however, as it was addressed to me but the name of the sender was not enclosed. It was a British Red Cross food parcel, so I think it was probably sent as an invalid-comforts parcel on the instructions of someone who had my welfare at heart.

The Middle East war was turning our way as General Montgomery was hounding the German General Rommel. Benghazi was 'evacuated according to plan' by the Germans on 30 December, news which was received with joy at the camp. It was good to realise that the Australian and British troops were executing a large scale manoeuvre which I felt sure would be accomplished again. Little did we realise that we were to see yet another great German advance, almost to Alexandria, before we were to drive the Germans right out of Africa.

The next night, being New Year's Eve, No. 1 Hut was the scene of a party and concert as we all welcomed in the New Year, with hopes that it would turn out to be better than its predecessor.

As the wine began to work the boys started singing and soon we had a competition going between the nations present.

'Come on, Red,' called Quinny to New Zealander Red Breckon, 'give us a haka.'

Red complied and jumped on our table. He got more and more worked up until with a great flourish he leaped into the air and hit his head on the low ceiling thus knocking himself out temporarily.

As two or three of the boys were stacking Red into the corner to recover, Rocky Trites called out, 'What have the Aussies got to offer apart from 'Waltzing Matilda', which everyone knows?'

In answer to that taunt Herbie Crump and I were up on the table in no time singing 'Click go the Shears' with enthusiasm, accompanied by sheep noises.

Not to be outdone, Quinny and Rocky and Suggy gave a discordant rendition of 'The Maple Leaf Forever', which was followed by Jock Alexander and Freddie Woods, accompanied by many other Brits, singing with gusto 'Roll out the Barrel'.

Eventually we got to sleep at 3.30 am. So now we were in a New Year — 1942 — a year which most of us thought (with our false optimism) would mark the end of our prison life. A lottery was run and it is interesting to note that the average month prisoners chose for the end of the war was June 1942!

CHAPTER 15
A DISMAL YEAR, 1942

As part of our 1942 innovations, a special clandestine news service was instigated by the prisoners and conducted in a manner similar to modern radio announcements. Freddie Woods and his satellite, Dick Whittingham, daily visited each hut in turn to announce the news of the day, as gleaned from varying sources, reliable and doubtful.

'News up, chaps!' Freddie would say after checking to make sure that the hut was properly secure from snooping German guards. 'Good news today. Montgomery has driven Rommel's forces east from Tobruk and it seems that Rommel is on the back foot at the moment. On the other hand the Germans have made some gains on the Russian front, though nowhere near what they claim. We'll have the BBC news again for you tomorrow. Let's hope Montgomery can keep going.'

This was really by way of an organised attempt to subdue the rumour mongers and quell the sources of 'duff gen' and was partially successful in achieving its objective. News filtered through each day of the reversal of the German forces and the gradual but slow advance of the Russians on the eastern front. Food rations for POWs were reduced shortly after this and the meagre allowance dwindled perceptibly till we fell to wondering how we would exist were we compelled to live on German POW rations alone. We also suspected that part of the meat ration for the prisoners found its way into the soup issued to the German guards.

The morning of 7 January dawned bright and clear. The ground was frozen hard beneath our feet and the water hung from the ablutions block in thick white icicles. During our breakfast we were interrupted and assembled outside. Another search was on! With every article of our belongings in Red Cross boxes under our arms we formed a straggling line of grumbling prisoners. We were warned that anything that was left in the huts would be confiscated, whether it be military or private.

89

No. 4 Hut was the first to be searched and as soon as the boys were all out we were marched to the Guard Room outside the compound and there halted. Four were then taken into the Guard Room to be frisked. Surplus socks and underclothing were withheld and the four men allowed to leave the Guard Room by a second door. There they were detained by two guards to prevent further intercourse with their friends until the search of the whole barrack had been completed. We were then marched back to our hut where we were left to grumble about the search and survey the remains of our long since cold breakfast.

Each hut was searched in turn and by nightfall the camp had been completely searched. The results of the Germans' labours were certainly not negligible. Forty unopened cans of foodstuffs had been found in the roof of No. 1 Hut and several maps had been discovered on persons.

From then onwards, our previous comparative freedom was denied us. The old system of locking doors at night was reverted to and the almost forgotten practice of queuing up for the latrine was recommenced, more from necessity than from inclination. The guards were greeted with a stony silence, such times as they ventured to speak. Feeling ran high in the camp; there was a general 'hate session' on, as many of us had been deprived of articles of clothing, the loss of which was felt acutely in the ensuing severe nights.

Mike had been taken to the local gaol for tearing up his pullover in the face of the commandant, and we all settled into bed that night in a restless, indignant mood, only to be further provoked by an argument which broke out between two rival sections in the hut.

Fed by the short tempers of all and sundry, it soon had the hut in an uproar.

'I'm going to complain to the Red Cross and to the German General Berger who is responsible for the treatment of prisoners,' said Bingham. 'These actions contravene the Geneva Convention. I'm sure the commandant is exceeding his authority though the discovery of hidden food to be used for escaping will be his excuse. The treatment of our clothing and personal effects is another thing! I'll make as big a fuss as I can tomorrow.'

Some suggestions for a hunger strike were soon dismissed as ridiculous under the present circumstances and most of the prisoners were resigned to putting up with the commandant's actions until authorities higher up forced a return to reasonable conditions of confinement according to the Geneva Convention.

A few days later Pat Ward returned from the hospital and brought with him some good news regarding the situation in Russia, which was improving daily from our point of view.

Some of the Russian troops, however, were supposed to have deserted and flown to Germany. Tripoli had been taken, which showed a further German advance in the Middle East. During that time a rumour found birth in the camp to the effect that Australia had been invaded by the Japanese and for one horrible day I found myself wondering whether or not there was any truth in it.

Two nights later we began the first of a series of bi-weekly talks. They were more or less impromptu and embraced the various jobs of the speakers before the war. It was a good scheme, and superseded the general knowledge bee, which was becoming a trifle overworked. By now the weather was steadily becoming colder and colder. Ice appeared in white frosty coatings on the walls of the hut and the ground was frozen hard underfoot. Trouble was experienced with the water system and even when the flow was uninterrupted, the wash-house itself gleamed with a myriad of glistening icicles as the water froze immediately on contact with the air. Outside activity was limited and most of the time was spent in the huts, either sleeping or playing bridge.

At six o'clock on the morning of 20 January, sleepy-eyed, munching a slab of toast, I walked briskly through the stalag gates in the crisp snow, accompanied by Taffy Owens and an armed guard. It was not yet light and a quiet, gloomy mantle rested on the land as we strode quickly towards the railway station, our breath condensing in frosty white clouds, our clogs ringing with a hollow thud on the frozen cobblestones. We were bound for Cottbus, a larger town some 40 miles distant, to undergo an examination by a specialist; Taffy for his eyes and I for my chest wound, which was still discharging. The visit, taking all day as it did, provided a welcome break in the monotonous stalag existence. We were back again by nightfall, having completed a little trading with some Frenchmen, but failed in our attempt to obtain some 'gen' (news).

By 30 January, the freezing spell had broken somewhat and a thaw began. Interaction between the huts increased. Some newly arrived sporting equipment was produced and indoor games were organised. A boxing match, the first of a series, was arranged and staged before a gathering of the camp, in No. 3 Hut. It met with great success and though actual ring conditions could not be faithfully reproduced some good bouts were arranged. Needless to say there were a few swollen noses and black eyes to be seen around the camp for a few days afterwards.

About this time, at noon one day, we were drawn outdoors by the sight of 18 Stukas passing overhead in loose formation, in all probability heading for the Eastern Front. This, of course, we interpreted as a good sign — 'badly needed reinforcements'. On 8 February we received another visit from a Red Cross representative.

He was anxious to pass on to us some good news and he assembled a group of us to explain a new education scheme for prisoners. He said, 'This scheme is designed to enable prisoners who wish to study while a prisoner to do so. We're going to send textbooks to camps for this purpose and prisoners will be able to enrol in institutions which give external courses.'

Jock Alexander broke in with, 'What about exams?'

The rep replied, 'Accredited teachers and supervisors will be appointed in camps and exam papers will be sent through the Red Cross. They will then be collected by the Red Cross and sent to the appropriate examining institutions.'

'And where will we sit the exams?' asked Quinny.

'The Germans will provide facilities for exam supervision,' came the reply. 'They are quite keen to get this scheme running as soon as possible.'

This scheme, if successful in practice, would prove a boon to all those prisoners of war who were previously studying for diplomas and public exams. From the German point of view it would perhaps direct attention away from thoughts of escape to thoughts of future qualifications. Of course, it did not always work that way. For example, I completed a

Chapter 15

Certificate in Social Science from Oxford University and a Bachelor of Science and Economics degree from London University while also escaping three times.

On 11 February we all received a blow in the way of news and felt down in the dumps for some time. Singapore had fallen — a disaster which we had thought well-nigh impossible. It must be remembered that every scrap of disheartening news was doubly hard for us as POWs as our main thoughts in life were centred on when the war would end. All talk, actions and thoughts had behind them the shadow of the boat that was to take us home.

Gloom settled over the camp. The Brits had never considered the possibility of Singapore, their bastion of the east, falling to the Japanese. The fact was that the Japanese soldiers were adept at jungle warfare and were good tacticians. They swept down rapidly through Vietnam, Cambodia, Thailand and Malaysia before taking Singapore by surprise. The Brits could not believe it. Many of them had brothers and friends in the British armed forces and were apprehensive about their fate. This was the beginning of the dismal year when most of the news coming from the various theatres of war was distressing to the kriegies (kriegsgefangeners — war prisoners), especially since communication with home was slow and halting. Anything that might prolong the end was a hard blow.

Following the fall of Singapore came news that the German battleships *Scharnhorst* and *Gneisnau* (which we had tried to bomb on our third sortie) had sneaked out of Brest and sailed north up the English Channel in foul weather to the North Sea, finally arriving at their destination comparatively unscathed. The RAF used mostly torpedo-carrying Swordfish aircraft, which were no match for the German fighters protecting the ships. With the loss of 65 British planes, it certainly seemed that the Germans had put it over us on this occasion, and they capitalised on it in their papers for weeks.

Not very long afterwards I was sent to Kirchain for a brief medical examination and 24 hours later was packing frantically. I was at last going to the Spremburg hospital to undergo treatment for the wound in my chest which was still open after 10 months. I had received comparatively short notice and so followed a day of frantic clothes drying and packing as I had just washed some shirts and socks. We had been issued with Red Cross parcels the previous day and I set about selling my foodstuffs for cigarettes because it was forbidden to carry food to the hospital. I disposed of most of it and, after accepting numerous messages for the boys already there, set out in the early hours of the morning of 25 February, heavily laden with Red Cross boxes containing my belongings.

The journey to Spremburg took half a day and was not particularly enjoyable because of the amount of clothes I was compelled to carry. However, I arrived there safely and was soon installed in a ward with Reg Thoburn, a fighter pilot from our stalag who had been there for five months with a cannon wound in his leg. Two others were already in the hospital — Alan Bull, an Aussie fighter pilot, and Dave Allen, a New Zealander who was later repatriated.

The hospital at Spremburg, which lay in a picturesque glen in the forest, was for the treatment of French, Belgian and Yugoslav prisoners and we four were the only Allied airmen there. Our stalag was too small to boast a hospital of its own. I was soon settled in as a bed patient and got down to some study and writing, rejoicing once more in the gentle caress of soft, white linen and a spring mattress. A few days before I had left the stalag, German Corporals Miller and Plutart, the interpreters, had been posted elsewhere and two new interpreters had taken their place. We were somewhat dubious about whether the standard of their work would be above or below that of their predecessors. So when I received four letters on the second day in hospital, I was agreeably surprised. It proved that at least the mail, our biggest source of concern, was being well handled.

On 5 March news came through of the first RAF raid on Paris and it was received in the hospital with varying degrees of feeling. A few — a very small minority — were violent in their abuse of the RAF. They shouted, 'The RAF are murderers! Bombing our lovely city and killing our women and children and destroying our beautiful buildings and churches. I hope the Germans shoot them down. They are not friends of ours.' These outbursts led to fights between groups of French soldiers themselves and the atmosphere in the camp was quite uncomfortable for a few days.

Five days later Taffy Owens, who had gone with me to Cottbus, arrived at the hospital for treatment to his eyes and, to our joy, brought with him some Red Cross parcels. To me, however, the arrival of Taffy and the accompanying food was of little moment for my wound had rapidly healed and I was due to return to the stalag in two days' time. The others sympathised with me over my early departure, which had been somewhat unexpected.

'Bad luck, Alex,' said Taffy. 'Things are not so crash hot back at the camp right now. The commandant is on one of his punishment rampages at the moment and life is certainly a lot better here than back there. But no doubt I shall be rejoining you soon.'

Imagine then, the surprise of all of us, but particularly of Alan and Dave, when we were informed that they would also accompany me on the following day. To use an air force expression, there followed 'bags of panic' — hurried packing, frantic washing of soiled linen and hasty trading — but by nightfall everything was ready for our departure on the morrow. I left the hospital with no regrets. It had been a nice change but I was glad to get back to the congenial atmosphere of the stalag. We had very little 'gen' to offer the boys. I noticed no change in the camp but the other two, who had been away since Christmas, noticed an alteration in the exterior and the interior aspects of the camp. The one peculiarity I did notice was what might have been called a premature reversion to second childhood. I doubt whether Shakespeare himself could have visualised such behaviour in men who were in the prime of life, but the fact remains that when I arrived back at the camp I found men behaving in a singularly strange manner.

A lot of the prisoners had become gunmen from the wild and woolly west, and would draw on the slightest provocation. One had only to enter one of the huts and he would immediately be covered from behind and from the beds. Gun duels were a common occurrence and some of the boys became remarkably quick on the draw. Not only was the cowboy element strongly in evidence but there was also a reversion to several other of our childhood pastimes.

Boat sailing was, I think, the most popular — the crude drain from the ablutions block provided an ideal watercourse. The method adopted was to block the flow of water at a point near the wash-house. The boats (crudely carved blocks of wood) were then placed in the gradually swelling reservoir formed by the water. At the signal from the starter the obstruction (a common garden spade) was removed and the water surged forward to the accompaniment of many excited cries, carrying with it the boats. These periods of childishness proved brief, however, and soon the camp returned to normal, gun duels and boat races becoming mere memories.

On 19 March I received a guitar from the YMCA and that afternoon, with the help of a violin, another guitar and a makeshift bass (constructed from a length of strong cord, a large jam tin and a wooden pole) we had a rhythm session, which became a regular daily occurrence. Spring was now here and the fine days drew the boys out of the huts to the playing field. The German glider school recommenced operations in the adjoining field and the young would-be pilots could be seen throughout the day, gliding noiselessly around the field, a sight which filled us with envy.

Then, on 26 March, we staged a grand spring cleaning, partly because the camp needed it and partly because we were expecting a visit from the Graf von Spremburg, the German Inspector-General of prison camps. The hut was completely cleared and the floors and walls washed, an operation which took a whole day. True to schedule, the general arrived the following day and inspected our barracks, seeming surprised at the number of persons to each hut. He brought a few points to the attention of the commandant but nothing more was heard of his visit and life continued as before.

The steady inflow of books from the Red Cross gave us a comprehensive selection and our library now looked quite healthy. Cigarettes and private food parcels were now coming through, though only for those with connections in England or America. We five Australians had to resign ourselves to fate and the charitable disposition of our friends. A letter received from Miss Ida Marx by Herb Crump, an Adelaide Wop/ AG, did nothing to improve matters.

The general tone of the letter implied that as prisoners we were useless airmen and could not really expect much service from the staff of Australia House; there were more important things to attend to. When we moved to other camps and met other Aussies, there did not seem to be one Aussie who had not heard of Ida Marx of Australia House and vowed to tell her exactly what he thought of her and her attitude to prisoners of war.

On 4 April we took our first walk, a stroll to Doberlug which lay two miles or so to the south of our camp. The day was fine and we were permitted the use of Red Cross boots for the stroll.

'I'd almost forgotten what a luxury it is,' said Suggy, 'to wear boots after the clogs the Jerries have forced on us.'

'Yeah,' chipped in Herbie, 'I'd almost forgotten what flowers look like too, and as for pretty young girls — well, I leave it to your imagination.'

'Trouble is,' said Ginger, 'It makes you realise what you're missing. The sooner that boat takes us home the better.'

We visited an old church dating from the 13th century, and were given a brief history of the structure and its surroundings by the interpreter. When we returned we were quite exhausted and pleased to find a keg of beer awaiting us. It was a habit to pay a certain amount of English cigarettes for a glass of beer. In fact it was about this time that the trading with the Germans grew to such proportions that it became necessary to control it by issuing a list of minimum prices for our goods. We had formed this system of trading to supply us with those things we needed but which were not issued to us, such as cooking utensils, cigarette lighters, notebooks and extra food. A small amount of our good quality Red Cross food, soap, chocolate and coffee had a phenomenal trading value, so we availed ourselves of the opportunity to supplement our larder.

On 12 April we received an addition to our complement at Stalag IIIE. An army corporal, a parachutist, arrived from Frankfurt after having been captured in Yugoslavia and interrogated in Berlin. He had gone through a number of exciting experiences and, being just recently captured, could give us the latest 'gen'. Later he was to be my escape partner.

A week or so later we were told that we would soon be moved to another camp, a recently built one, where we would find many other RAF prisoners. It was part of a scheme to concentrate all RAF prisoners in one large camp and I found myself wondering whether I would meet any of my crew whom I had not seen for a year.

The twenty-third of April was an important day in my life. It was my 21st birthday. It was the same as every other day for all the kriegies except me. Although for me it was a special day nothing much of any consequence happened except for one kind gesture by a fellow prisoner I had barely met. Harry Calvert did not know me but had heard that it was my birthday that day.

I was sitting on my bed trying to decide what I could do to make this day different in some way from all the other days when Cal poked his head in the door. Harry Calvert was a Canadian whose father was the Canadian Governor-General. He was older than most of us and had already earned a name as the camp's most successful trader. He was adept at getting what he wanted from the German guards in exchange for what he didn't want. He was a close buddy of Suggy with whom he later escaped.

He said to me, 'I heard it's your birthday today.'

'That's right, Cal,' I replied. 'I'm 21 today.'

He stroked his well-trimmed beard. 'I thought so,' he said, 'so I bought you a small present to brighten up the day.' In his hand he held an egg; the first egg I had seen for 12 months.

'Happy birthday, Aussie,' he said with a smile as he put the egg in my hand. As he retreated to his hut with my thanks ringing in his ears I had to reflect on human nature.

The egg was a truly rare morsel in the rather austere atmosphere of the stalag in those early days. He had acquired it by trading with a German. Together with my lump of hard German rye bread and my small measure of ersatz margarine and jam it made my day, and I will never forget the generosity from someone who hardly knew me but considered that the significance of the occasion demanded a gesture of compassion.

CHAPTER 16
THE TUNNEL, 1942

The news of our impending shift was rather alarming in one way as it meant a hastening of work on a tunnel which we had been constructing for some months. We did not know the exact date on which we were to move but we knew it would be in the very near future so we were in doubt whether we would be able to complete the tunnel and escape from it before we were due to be moved.

Planning had got underway by Christmas 1941 to dig the tunnel leading north to an empty field across which an escape could be made. The entrance to the tunnel was beneath the floor of one of the huts.

Five months later, in May 1942, after much laborious digging in the sandy soil the tunnel was nearly complete, with perhaps another 30 feet or so to go. The tunnel was crudely lit, the darkness broken here and there by small tins containing pyjama cords soaked in margarine. That was the only form of lighting we had. The tunnel was shored up on the top and sides by bed boards to prevent collapses as unfortunately the soil was rather sandy. The dimension of the tunnel allowed a person only to crouch down and this became very enervating and painful after a while. For this reason digging shifts were shorter than ideal. Because of the confined pace the tunnel also became unpleasantly hot.

The sweating kriegies worked their shifts in claustrophobic silence, gasping to get their share of the somewhat foul-smelling air filtering down through the two air holes that had been dug for ventilation. Cardboard boxes were filled with sand dug out from the face with empty food tins, and passed down a line of crouching men through their legs. This provided the delivery system for the spoil, which was distributed surreptitiously around the outside compound. The kriegies waiting at the entrance would fill socks and linen bags with sand, suspend them inside their trouser legs and then walk around the compound slowly releasing the sand as they went.

The longer the tunnel became the worse were the working conditions, due to lack of adequate fresh air, and the harder it became to hide the spoil. From the time we heard of our impending shift on 20 April until 10 May we worked like Trojans. The two ventilation holes had thin 10-foot shafts to the surface where they were loosely covered with rocks. The air was very poor. Shifts could work only for half an hour or so at a time because the air was so foul. On one occasion the fellow in front of me passed out and we had to haul him out feet first.

Many in the camp had laboured long and hard over that tunnel. At 42 metres (138 feet) it was, we subsequently discovered, the longest tunnel through which a successful escape had been made. It was also one of the most confined for it was only one bed board (approximately 3 feet) square. Soon we ran out of bed boards. As it was, most prisoners slept on corrugated mattresses as their bed boards gradually disappeared over several months before the final breakout. We could not use more or the Germans would eventually have noticed their absence and become suspicious. As the tunnel progressed from under the floor of No. 4 Hut towards the perimeter wire and the adjoining flying field over which we were going to make our escape, the problem of sand disposal became acute. Two Canadians with previous mining experience directed the overall operation and the work was arranged in two shift periods, morning and afternoon.

The construction of the tunnel was not without incident. There was the occasion when the face collapsed and wild panic ensued.

'What's happened?' called Herbie as the kriegies started backing up against one another in haste.

'The face of the tunnel has collapsed!' replied Taffy, who was further up the line of diggers, 'And it's filling the tunnel with dust.'

'Back up! Back up!' yelled Herbie as the dust came billowing down the line to the accompaniment of coughing and sneezing.

Then there was the time when a visiting German general kicked idly at a rock which was sitting loosely on the ground to camouflage the one air hole we had drilled at that stage. Then there was the day when two face workers could not get out quickly enough to appear on a sudden roll call and had to be covered for when counting began. To this were added the doubts and differences of opinion as to exactly where the tunnel had got to on the day of the proposed breakout, and the final drawing of lots for positions in the breakout queue.

Everything was going reasonably well when crisis and consternation struck. In early May we were informed that we would be shifted to the other camp within a week. The chief tunnellers (Canadians Harry Calvert and Don Sugden) were called upon for an accurate assessment. Was the tunnel now beyond the wire or was it still within the confines of the camp?

Cal finally came up with their answer: 'To the best of our knowledge we think that we'll be level with the wire in about two days provided we can step up our rate of digging. Then we'll need about another three days to make a safe breakout.'

We hoped that their measurements were accurate. With the impending shift to another camp drawing close it was now or never. There were risks involved, with the opening so close to the wire and with trigger-happy guards in their towers overlooking the territory we had to traverse before we made cover. But there was little hesitation in making the decision — we would go.

The kriegies gathered together in small groups to discuss the situation. Jock Alexander, the camp leader, said, 'Tomorrow we'll increase the number of digging parties and the length of their shifts. We want an all-out effort — it's now or never. Tomorrow I'll also call for more volunteers to distribute the soil. And we'll have to monitor progress more closely now so that we know exactly where we are. The Germans haven't yet given us a deadline so we must be prepared to act quickly.'

We had suffered many setbacks in the form of occasional hard soil, inspection parades which shortened our length of working time, foul air which caused our candles to fail and more than one of the men to faint, windless days which left our air holes almost useless, and finally the despatch of the first group of men to the new camp at Sagan which reduced our workforce. But in spite of it all we finished the five-month task with six hours to spare. It was coincidence that I had been exactly a year in Germany to the day; in fact I got out of the tunnel within an hour of the time we were shot down.

SHOT DOWN

The decision having been made and the deadline having been set by the Germans, furious activity began among the would-be escapees — organising individual escape kits, drawing lots for places in the queue, writing letters to be posted home by friends if the worst happened, packing food which had been hoarded for this venture over previous weeks and so on. The would-be escapees (52 out of 184 were able to go) were silent on the breakout night, wrapped in their thoughts and now facing the reality of risking their lives for freedom. We all knew that the German guards would not hesitate to fire at an escaping prisoner.

At 11.30 pm, with charcoal blackened faces and hands, we began to enter the tunnel at regular time intervals, making sure that the escaping gear strapped on our backs did not cause obstruction and that we made no noise as we crouched in the confines of the ever-so small passage — deathly, apprehensive silence, heavy breathing and muffled voices from up front. At one point there was a rumour that dogs were at the tunnel entrance. We were all keyed-up, apprehensive — pulses racing, adrenaline pumping and wanting to get it over with.

The tunnel was breached around midnight and Calvert and Sugden were first out followed by Jock Alexander, our camp leader. Thereafter it was by ballot. I was number 11. Some 52 prisoners altogether got out. That was not the total number hoping to make the break but rather the number of successful escapees — the others were trapped in the camp when the tunnel hole was discovered. We were among the lucky ones and were out within 30 minutes of the first breakout. The exit hole was, fortunately, outside the wire but not very far from it; in fact it was dangerously close but because of the timing it had to be now or never and the risk of being discovered had to be taken. Fortunately, the German guards in the towers were looking into the compound and the German perimeter guard patrolled inside the wire and it was some time before he glanced outside and the broken earth was discovered barely 16 feet away. At that point all hell broke loose.

CHAPTER 17
ON THE LOOSE, 1942

We emerged in our twos and threes, faces and hands blackened, knives, other implements and rations concealed in our clothing. We had to crawl across 100 yards of open field to the relative safety of the woods beyond. That crawl will ever remain indelibly printed in my memory. We could not look back but had to move forward in silence, in the moonlight, making as little movement as possible. At any moment a guard in a watchtower might be taking a bead on the back of my head. My tongue and mouth were so dry that I literally could not swallow. All the saliva was drained from me as adrenaline pumped through my veins to prepare me for whatever effort might be called for. It seemed to me that I spent about an hour crawling and waiting for that fateful shot, but in truth it was probably no more than 15 minutes.

As it was, it all passed uneventfully and Chip, Wingy and I gathered ourselves together once we were under cover and sped off through the woods to put as much distance as possible between us and the camp before the disturbed earth was discovered and the inevitable happened.

At the edge of the forest in a steady drizzle of rain we took stock of the layout. The forest was quite thick and thus would offer good cover. But the dense forest made it easy to lose one's bearings. 'South is this way,' said Chip pointing at right angles to the camp.

'I agree,' said Wingy and we took off without further delay, each of us trying to make sure we did not deviate from our line.

Our hideout that morning, under a fallen branch in the forest, was not the best but we managed to last out the day and got underway as soon as night fell, our clothes having dried out during the afternoon. We pushed on through forests all that night, heading south by the stars, and finally picked a hideout — a small nook in a wood. We camouflaged it with branches and leaves as day was breaking and then settled down to sleep after a small meal.

SHOT DOWN

Before setting out on the second night we took a wash at a nearby stream which was running through the centre of a large field. As we were cleaning our teeth an aeroplane flew overhead, turned and switched on its landing lights as it headed in our direction. It lit up the field and my heart leapt until I realised that it would have been impossible for him to see us motionless near the stream. Unwittingly we had stopped near the flight path of a flying field. We took no chances and moved out of that area without further delay. After a strenuous night's walking we selected our hideout in dense forest by a large stream. There was a considerable amount of dry grass hanging around and we gathered it together to lie in the bottom of some large holes which we came across — evidence of recent tree-felling activity.

During the day we were startled by a hoarse barking noise coming from a thicket nearby. 'Quiet. There's a dog in that thicket,' said Wingy.

'No, it's a deer,' whispered Chip.

'Whatever it is,' I whispered back, 'Let's keep quiet and cover ourselves. No talking until we're sure it's gone.'

A forester passed within 20 feet of us late in the afternoon, but we lay absolutely still with hearts beating furiously until we heard his footsteps dying away in the distance. We finished off our bulk food that day and were now down to our meagre rations of cheese and chocolate and whatever we might manage to scrounge in the fields or elsewhere. At this time of the year there was very little edible food to be obtained in the countryside and we could find nothing at all to help us on our way.

On that third night we skirted around a factory and discovered a vegetable plot in the yard of a nearby house which we presumed was occupied by the factory manager. After spending some time reconnoitring to ensure there were no dogs or other hazards, we entered the garden and proceeded to strip it. The action which gave us the most mirth at the time, and the most pain subsequently, was to relieve the gardener of his small plot of mature rhubarbs. We carefully cut off the stalks at the bottom and the leaves at the top and placed all the leaves back on the stumps so that the whole plot would appear in the morning to suddenly have shrunk during the night! When we later ate the raw rhubarb we all had the most violent stomach pains.

Chapter 17

'I think it was that rhubarb,' said Wingy. 'We didn't cook it and we should have known better than to eat raw rhubarb. We're going to have be a bit more careful in the future. These things slow us down and we haven't got all that much in the way of food we can fall back on. We're beginning to run out of time.'

'At least,' I said, 'if we can travel south quickly enough there will be more fruit and vegetables available for the picking in the warmer climate. I think we might have to consider train-jumping to speed up our progress.'

But soon after we moved off on the fourth night, I took ill and had to be helped along by Chip while Wingy carried my pack; it was made from a blanket and contained all my provisions with the exception of an emergency tin containing chocolate, which I always carried on my person. Our progress that night was almost negligible and we went to earth long before daybreak as I was too ill to go further. I brought up all the food I had eaten for the past three days (which was precious little) and fell asleep where I lay in the sand. The illness must have been caused by bad water as we had drunk from streams and drains with not much regard for taste or impurities. Beggars can't be choosers.

During the fifth day we were constantly disturbed by aircraft activity overhead and intermittent explosions nearby. The awful truth finally dawned on us that in the dark we had inadvertently gone to earth on an aircraft bombing range. In the night we had trudged across a large sandy waste in the darkness of a cloudy sky and finally holed up in a small clump of bushes in a slight dip in the sand. We thought that it was so deserted that we would be safe during the day. How wrong we were! It was much later, when a carload of Luftwaffe officers stopped nearby, in the afternoon, to plot the positions of the bomb bursts (they were so close that we could clearly hear their conversation), that we realised the explosions were made by practice bombs dropped by the trainee pilots. The irony of it struck us as we realised that all day we had been receiving what we had been used to dishing out the previous year.

The officers finally left and we breathed freely again. We experienced some breathless moments late in the afternoon of the same day when four foresters presumably on survey work crossed over the sand plain, heading straight for us. When no more than 10 yards from the bush where I was crouched, they veered to the left to avoid it and passed along the side of our hideout. Their voices died away as they disappeared down a small incline and left us lying absolutely still, breathless, bathed in perspiration, pulses pounding.

That night we took a shave and a bathe in a nearby lake then set forth again. From the landmarks we passed every now and then, I could see we were dead on track and at last we felt reasonably safe as we had managed to last out for four days. Hiding out in a deserted house in the forest and chatting over a cigarette, we reflected on our position.

'That swim was good,' said Chip. 'I really do feel like a free man now. It's a great feeling.'

'I wonder how the other chaps are going,' mused Wingy. 'I thought we might have seen some of them by now. Anyhow, good luck to them.'

'I think we should push our good luck and have a go at the trains tomorrow,' I said. 'Our food's starting to run low.'

Although train-jumping was hazardous in the extreme, we needed to increase our rate of progress south and this was the only way. We had reached the stage when we were compelled to crawl up any steep slope on our hands and knees, not having enough energy to walk. Our rests were becoming longer and more frequent and it was obvious that we would have to hasten our pace if we were to reach our objective before our food ran out completely.

We were headed for Yugoslavia. On the first night of our escapade, Chip had said to us, 'I have a radio hidden in Yugoslavia. We could head there. When I was dropped by the RAF to make contact with partisans commanded by General Michailovich our party ran into some Germans. Some of us were killed and I was taken prisoner. But I hid the radio first.'

I said, 'Can you remember where you hid it?'

He said, 'Yeah, I plotted exactly where I hid it. I'll be able to find it again if we can just get there.'

Wingy said excitedly, 'So ... we could contact London! Providing the radio hasn't been discovered or damaged of course.'

Chapter 17

'That's the plan,' said Chip. 'If we can get to it we could either be in the friendly hands of the partisans or back in London very quickly.'

To us it seemed to offer better prospects for an early return than to try to make our way across Germany and France to Spain or north through Denmark to Sweden, both of them escape routes that were familiar to the Germans.

We got underway as soon as possible on the fifth night and early the following morning we reconnoitred a railway siding with a view to jumping a train heading south. We discussed how we would go about boarding it.

'We've got to make sure of the train's direction,' I said, 'and we must get a goods train that's just gathering speed as it comes out of a junction or one that's labouring uphill and travelling slow enough for us to board. To try and board a train that's going too fast would be disaster. We have to spread out and each take an adjoining truck so that when we're on board we can assemble at the central point and remain one tight bunch.'

The manoeuvre worked successfully and two hours later we were clinging precariously between the carriages of a fast-travelling goods train. We had run alongside and jumped the train while it was labouring slowly up a long slope. After breasting the slope, it soon gathered speed but 30 minutes or so later began to slow down again. We found ourselves in the central rail junction of a large manufacturing town. We hadn't planned on this.

Our first attempt at train-jumping very nearly proved to be our last because as the train stood panting in the centre of the well-lit junction a soldier with rifle on shoulder could be seen walking the length of the train, checking each guard cabin. While the train was travelling we had climbed around from our precarious perches above the couplings we leapt onto then opened the door and let ourselves into a guard's cabin, hoping we were safe for a lengthy journey. Perhaps we had been spotted clinging to the van by a railwayman as the goods train entered the junction. In any event, the guard was looking in each guard's cabin as he went along and discovery seemed imminent and inescapable.

The guard reached our cabin and tried to open the door. Wingy was nearest to the door and he held it tightly so that it did not move and the guard could not open it. While Wingy held on to the handle of his door Chip opened the door on the other side and he and I jumped out and ran for our very lives followed closely by Wingy, who had released his door at the last moment. It was a large marshalling yard and we ran awkwardly across several sets of rails in our cumbersome clogs. In what appeared to our scared eyes to be almost broad daylight we jumped over the rails, expecting a shout and a shot in the back any second. Actually the war-time lighting was not very bright and this undoubtedly helped us.

Miraculously nothing happened, and to this day we can't explain it. As we ran, Wingy caught his clog in a rail and ripped it off his foot but hardly faltered in his stride as he bent down to retrieve it. We clattered across the rails making a great noise with our wooden clogs, expecting to be caught at any moment, but somehow we were spared. Soon we reached the high brick wall surrounding the rail yard and with our adrenaline working overtime literally flew up and over it to flop breathlessly against the other side in the dark. We took stock and found that Wingy's clog was repairable and that we had not lost any of our possessions. We just could not believe our luck not to have been seen by anyone else let alone the guard, who we think must certainly have seen us making off into the night. Maybe he thought we were harmless hoboes or maybe he was scared too.

The problem now was how to get out of the town we were in without being apprehended. We were plumb in the middle and it took us half an hour or so of walking to get clear and into a good hiding spot. Several times as we walked along in the night I muttered greetings in German to passers-by, but we did not attract attention. Mostly the streets were deserted as it was cold and misty and rather unpleasant to be outside. Although the night was young, we were rather shaken by our close call and decided to hole up for the remainder of the night and reconsider our strategy within the options available.

Despite our dangerous baptism, train-jumping won out and we decided that our only hope was to press south on trains as quickly as possible.

Chapter 17

'I'm not sure that's the right way to go,' said Chip. 'We bloody nearly got shot or captured. We should try to think up another way of travelling that's safer. Apart from the chances of getting shot you only have to misjudge the leap to the train and you end up a mangled mess on the rails.'

'True,' said Wingy. 'But what options do we have? We actually boarded our first train quite well and there's no reason we can't do it again. And the German guard was just a bit of bad luck. I think we have to keep to the trains if we're going to get anywhere.'

I agreed with Wingy and after discussing the situation during the remainder of the night we decided to continue with our train-jumping in the absence of a better alternative.

For the next three nights this is what we did. The pattern was to wait at the upward end of a long, preferably steep slope, and jump onto the trucks when they were at their slowest. We would then climb from truck to truck to converge on whoever was the central person and remain together for the night in the guard's cabin of the van we had chosen. Around an hour before dawn we would prepare to jump and then wait for a suitable slope to slow down the train. This would then give us enough time to find a nearby hiding place before day broke.

We did more or less the same thing on the ninth night after finishing off our rations, and by daybreak, as the result of an over-hasty decision to jump a train because we were running out of time, we found ourselves miles off track and unwilling to jump because the train was travelling too fast. Eventually it slowed sufficiently for us to risk jumping and then we were racing against time to find a suitable hideout before daybreak. There was little cover. It was a difficult task and we panted on desperately past treeless ploughed fields, our hope fading as the light became stronger. Eventually it became imperative that we should go to earth so we reluctantly selected a large hole in a ploughed field. It was none too good but the best to be obtained in an area which was almost devoid of trees. We had been free for 10 days when we were caught late that evening.

CHAPTER 18
RECAPTURED, 1942

We were congratulating ourselves on not having been seen throughout the day. We were not well hidden and we could hear farmers at work in the adjoining field. Then out of the dusk loomed the burly form of a forester sporting a shotgun. He stood on the edge of our hole and pointed it directly at my stomach and I figured that he could not miss at that range; in fact he could not miss even with a rifle or a hand gun at that range, so deciding rapidly that discretion was the better part of valour I gave up any idea of running for it.

'Hande hoch oder ich schiessen!' he barked. (Hands up or I will shoot!) 'Bewegen sie sich nicht. Wer bist du?' (Don't move. Who are you?)

'Wir sind Franzosisch gefangener,' I replied. 'Letzte nacht haben wir entkommen.' (We are French prisoners. We escaped last night.)

We had previously decided what our strategy would be if caught — we would not admit to being British airmen. So I immediately told our captor, in German, that we were escaped French prisoners. We spoke only French between ourselves. English was not spoken until we were in official hands. There was good reason for this. We knew that the RAF was now bombing Berlin, Hamburg, Cologne, Frankfurt and many other cities in the industrial complex, and that German civilians were beginning to maltreat — even lynch — Allied aircrew who had been shot down. Aircrew who landed by parachute into the centre of a large city were occasionally hanged from the nearest lamp post. German newspapers and ubiquitous posters proclaimed that women and children were being killed by the allied 'Luft Gangsters' and the civilians were conditioned to regarding aircrew as murderous bastards who concentrated on killing civilians. This was not the intention of the RAF, or indeed of the USAF, but there was no doubt that thousands of civilians were being killed and maimed every night and day. Some Germans were anxious to exact revenge for deaths in their families and took it out on downed aircrew.

Because of this we had agreed that we would not reveal our identity until we were in the hands of the German Luftwaffe (Air Force) or Wehrmacht (Army) who, we hoped, would treat us correctly as prisoners of war. It happened by extreme good fortune that our masquerade as escaped French soldiers was accepted by the forester quite readily as, unknown to us, a breakout had just taken place at a nearby camp for French prisoners which was within walking distance of our hiding place, and all the forest wardens in the area were on the lookout for escaped French prisoners. So although we were happy to be taken prisoner without any ugly or possibly fatal confrontation, our longer term luck had deserted us! Had the Frenchmen not broken out of their camp there would not have been a search and we may have gone undetected even though poorly hidden. We gathered up our bundles and walked to the nearby French camp, our captor following close on our heels, gun cocked. There we were interrogated, searched, given a wash and shave, and locked up in a cell for the night.

Recognising us as not from their camp they found an English-speaking officer to interrogate us.

'We are escaped prisoners from Stalag IIIE in Kirchain,' I said.

'I know,' he said much to our surprise. 'We know all about your escape. The news has spread over Germany. We will take you back to your stalag tomorrow.'

Apparently military and civilian units in all of central and southern Germany had been informed of the Kirchain breakout and told to keep a lookout. Every police station had a poster giving photos and descriptions of every escapee. I still have a copy. It reads as follows (translated).

GERMAN CRIMINAL POLICE LEAFLET
Given out from the State Police Centre in Berlin 13th May, 1942
Only for appointed German Authorities
A New Proclamation
English POW Airman Escape from the Kirchain Camp on 12th May, 1942.

SHOT DOWN

In the night of 12ᵗʰ May 1942, fifty-two English POW slipped away from Stalag IIIE Kirchain. They are young airmen (sergeants) aged from 20-30 years, healthy, athletic and very good constitutions, and almost all have slender sports figures (athletic). They are for the most part students, engineers, technicians and so on. Clothing: blue-grey English airmen uniforms without rank mark, nor fresh (i.e. dirty, unpressed). Captives without any head-wear, leather shoes with wooden soles or only stumps (remains of shoes), barefoot.

It is thought that the fugitives themselves have got other articles of clothing than provided or through theft on the way. The precise flight (escape) direction is at present still unknown. Ten of the escapees were in one neighbourhood 20–30 miles from Kirchain and certainly active under cover of darkness. It is hence reckoned that the fugitives themselves were by day in woods, secluded huts, or cart houses hidden and only in darkness their flight path continues.

The fugitives are (drawing to a close) with every step hindered. They are energetically searched for with leads from officials and particularly with reinforcements from rangers. It is also for the Chief District Administrator, Forest Administrator, Overseer of the Roads, Armed Forces, Local Field Police, for each to take their share of taking care.

Information and announcements from time to time are made from the Criminal Police of Berlin K-J-F, and news from this time forward given to the State Criminal Police C-2.

Even training aircraft were used in the first few days to try to locate prisoners on the move. The escape had caused quite a fuss which we had been completely unaware of.

Next day we were sent back to our old camp where we found most of our fellow escapees who had been caught before us. Fifty-two men had made the break and I made the 48th to be caught. Everyone was in a miserable frame of mind. We were waiting on the remaining four and the following day three were brought into the hut. That made a score of 51 caught and one killed.

Don Sugden and Calvert, the two Canadians, had escaped together and were doing well until they were caught on the tenth day. As he was being interrogated by his captor, Cal, who could speak no German and was standing with his hands raised, pointed to his socks and said, 'Can I keep my socks?' The instant reply of the guard was to shoot him where he stood. One bullet in the heart killed him instantly and left a disbelieving Suggy in a state of shock. This was the only casualty in the mass escape. The guard was never brought to justice despite intensive enquiries by Suggy after the war.

The breakout had given us a lot of experience on which to build future attempts. It had sent shock waves to Berlin, which had shaken the German prison camp administration and attracted the attention of the Gestapo itself. On the whole it was a good attempt, though we were hampered by our wooden clogs and ill-equipped for a lengthy escape from central Germany. We really did not stand much chance of getting out of Germany when we reflected on it. It was not a very professional job when compared with some later escapes from other camps. But it did give us an important morale boost and sense of triumph, however brief, to the escapees themselves and to their comrades. We had beaten the Germans!

The camp had been taken over by the Gestapo and they were not happy with the breakout, which showed flaws in the German security. The interrogation of recaptured prisoners was carried out by a Luftwaffe officer and a black-coated Gestapo official, both from Berlin. It began with the offer of a chair, cigarettes and a drink and these pleasantries continued in that vein throughout the interrogation despite our lack of cooperation.

'Sit down, sergeant,' began the Gestapo interrogating officer. 'Would you like a cigarette? We want to establish your identity before we release you to rejoin your fellow prisoners.' I accepted a cigarette and a drink that was offered at the same time.

'Name and number and rank please,' said the officer. 'We won't take long. We just need some information that I'm sure you can give us. Are you English or Australian or Canadian? How long have you been a prisoner? What were you flying when you were shot down? I notice you have some chocolate on you. How did you get it? You had some fresh vegetables on you too. Where did you get them? Was your escape easy? The knife you had — how did you get it? Did you find it easy to travel at night?'

The questions went on for a while but each one, apart from name rank and number, got an evasive answer or a flat 'Don't know'. The drinks dried up as the officer tired of the negatives and terminated the interrogation. We were taken to rejoin our comrades in the huts.

Many of us had been caught with knives and other forbidden possessions, clear evidence that the German guards had been trading with us. The Gestapo were anxious to bring them to justice, to clean up the trading that they knew was going on and to make an example by using harsh punishments. They tried to entice us to spill the beans and name the traders.

The interesting point in the whole interrogation process, which lasted over several days as recaptured escapees were brought in, was that not one person revealed the identity of the German traders. So the Gestapo were none the wiser after the interrogation process was completed. In the interim we received the royal treatment from our local army captors, who realised that we now held the power of life or death over them as the punishment for trading was very severe. It could result in the soldier being executed or being sent to the Russian front, which just about amounted to the same thing. As long as we withheld the vital information from the Gestapo we could demand almost anything from our German guards by exercising the simplest form of blackmail. We were fed better than ever before. The soups had more meat and vegetables and we realised what we had been missing.

The extent of the breakout, the consternation it caused within the military hierarchy and the civil reactions it led to within Germany, had made front page news. The skies seemed filled with light aircraft which had been taken off other duties to search for us. Police and wardens were continually on the lookout for people who looked like escaped prisoners. Those who tried moving by day were the first to be apprehended. We had improved our chances by opting to move only at night.

We had all been recaptured within 10 days. We had chalked up a few records, unwittingly, in our labours to seek a path to freedom. The total of 52 men to get out made it the largest breakout to that date (of the 52, all were recaptured, but Calvert was shot dead upon recapture). As well as the largest breakout it was the longest tunnel. The length of the tunnel was 42 metres (46 yards), making it longer than any tunnel in World War I and the longest so far in World War II. It was also the only tunnel from which all who escaped actually got away. Our new-found fame had preceded us and when we got to our new camp the Chief Escape Officer in the officers' compound sent a message of congratulations to us that said, 'Congratulations, chaps. You put on a really good effort and showed the Jerries they can't keep us in. Keep it up.'

Our new camp was Stalag Luft III, which was built solely to house air force prisoners. The German High Command had introduced a policy of segregating air force prisoners from those of the army and navy. The numbers of airmen being shot down and taken prisoner was mounting rapidly as the Allied air offensive grew in intensity. Airmen, because they operated over enemy territory, had a much higher risk of becoming prisoners and consequently were equipped with aids to escape such as silk maps sewn into the lining of their tunics, compasses which formed a collar stud, flying boots which could be converted into shoes and so on. And aircrew were conditioned to think in terms of escaping. The percentage of escapes from aircrew was much greater than that from army and navy personnel. Consequently German security was much tighter at the designated air force camps and, unlike in the army camps, no airman was allowed to work in the fields because opportunities to escape were easier.

CHAPTER 19
STALAG LUFT III: SAGAN, POLAND, 1942

We arrived at 6.30 pm on 1 June at Stalag Luft III, Sagan, Poland, the new big air force camp, scene of the Great Escape that took place two years later. We were searched then left in a new reception barrack, fenced off by barbed wire from the airmen in the main compound. Soon our old friends who had preceded us from IIIE gathered at the other side of the wire, among them Freddie who had with him my observer, Bill, and the rest of my crew, minus Andy. So at last we were all together again, even Bill whom I had left six months previously in the Frankfurt hospital, presumably headed for home.

As soon as we were allowed into the main compound the five of us got together to exchange news and at last I was able to piece together the remaining parts of the puzzle which had confronted me in the hospital.

I already knew how Bill had come out of our encounter with von Bonin but there were many questions I had to ask Dave Fraser about what had happened to me.

'I tried to eject sideways from my turret,' Dave said, 'but the hydraulics would not do the job so I tried to crawl into the cabin and get out that way. It was then that I saw you lying on the floor, obviously wounded. You had crawled almost to the escape hatch and I opened it so that we could get out. You seemed lethargic and unable to coordinate your efforts to jettison so I clipped your parachute on and pushed you out of the hatch. I saw you vanish into the night and caught a flash of white as the canopy of your parachute opened. Then I jumped myself.'

'Thank God you had to eject from inside the cabin,' I said. 'If the hydraulics had not been damaged I would have been left in the blazing aircraft. When we get back to Blighty I'll buy you a beer for that.'

Chapter 19

Of our captain, Andy, nothing had been heard — not one scrap of information that might give some clue to whether he was dead or still alive. After the war it was confirmed that he had parachuted into the Elbe and drowned.

There were many other Aussies in the camp, 33 in all, including some who had come over with me in the No.1 course from Australia. They gave me a lot of information regarding my old pals and my hometown, which was accepted greedily. Alan McSweyn, later to make a successful escape, Jock McKechnie and Clive Hall — all pilots — had been shot down while I was in hospital. As they had completed more operations than me they had been commissioned and therefore were in the officers' compound and thus separated from us, but we managed to exchange news with a barbed-wire fence between us.

We found that we were to remain permanently in the reception barrack owing to the rest of the blocks being filled, so we settled down, nailing up lockers, arranging beds and cleaning out the rooms. The beds were constructed in double tiers as distinct from the triple bunks of our previous stalag, and the rooms, being absolutely new, were much cleaner.

The camp held 2000 prisoners — officers and men; the officers living in a separate compound from the airmen. We were all guarded by Luftwaffe personnel. Sports equipment, gardening implements, two orchestras, a fire pool which could be used to swim in, and an extensive library gave us plenty of diversion and on the whole I liked the new camp much more than IIIE. In addition, we were treated reasonably by the Luftwaffe, which was certainly a change from our previous stalag where we had been guarded rather aggressively by the army.

On 27 May the Germans discovered a tunnel which some lads from another barrack had been digging. They also discovered the would-be escapists themselves in the tunnel and marched them off to gaol. A day later something I had been long expecting eventuated. I received 28 letters in one day from Australia, Canada, America, England and Scotland, and it took me a complete day and night to read and digest them. It was as though Christmas, New Year and Easter had all come at once as I travelled in my thoughts to those five countries to share news with my friends scattered over the globe.

Following closely on their heels came my first personal parcel from my Aunt Mary in Scotland, and I was now well off for clothes and toilet articles. Plenty of cigarettes began to roll in for the Canadians in our room and our only worry now was the most important one — food. There were, in our combine, four Canucks, three Anzacs, one Scotsman and two Englishmen, and we pooled all food and cigarettes. In this way, with two chief cooks, we managed to live well for a few days until our Red Cross parcels gave out. With the likelihood of the barrack soon filling up, as each successive batch arrived from Dulag we held a meeting to elect barrack officers. There were four positions to be filled and the men elected were to live in a small office at one end of the barrack.

Jock Alexander, the captain of our previous camp, was elected barrack leader and Don Sugden, a Canadian, his assistant. Ivan Quinn, another Canadian, filled the post of Red Cross clothing representative and I became the Red Cross food representative. I was responsible for taking delivery of the food parcels from the Germans when they came in from time to time and distributing them to the various combines. It was in this way that the four of us found ourselves in the office at the end of the hut. With a private stove to which was attached an oven which we had constructed from Red Cross tins, we thought ourselves quite well off.

On 8 June a large batch of new kriegies arrived from Dulag, most of whom had been shot down during a large raid on Cologne, forerunner to the mass raids which became quite frequent. The Cologne raid itself took place on 1 June and no fewer than 1000 planes had been over the target, coming in wave after wave throughout the night. The fresh prisoners, when taken through Cologne the following day, were amazed at the damage they saw and were glad to quit the city, as the civilians displayed unusual aggressiveness. This included lynching some of the aircrew who had come down by parachute.

Among those taken prisoner was Doug Watkins, who had been in my company in the 16th Battalion back in Perth, and who had still been there when news of my having been taken prisoner reached him. I found a billet for him in my hut where I proceeded to extract from him all news of my friends I had left behind. Soon after this I began to receive invalid comfort parcels, which were very welcome as we were out of Red Cross parcels. However, a day or so afterwards another food batch arrived, which kept the wolf from the door for a further fortnight.

Nothing much of interest happened until 22 June when we received the news that General Rommel had taken Tobruk after a short, fierce encounter. This was a blow to us and spirits fell in the camp as the German Army advanced towards Alexandria and threatened the Suez. That night, as we lay in our bunks after lights out, we could hear a great deal of shunting and truck movement on the rails which were 400 yards from the camp. As the trains clashed and rattled we could hear troops cheering and shouting; the Germans there seemed to be in very good spirits, no doubt resulting from the news of their favourite general's success in Africa. Shortly after this we heard that Anthony Eden had scooped the remaining shares of the Suez at the time that Alexandria was threatened.

On 23 June three officers escaped and got well away. The first inkling we had of anything amiss was six shots which pierced the night in quick succession. We strained our ears for any further sound but nothing more was heard and, dismissing it as a mistake on the part of one of the posterns (guards), some of whom seemed very nervous and light-fingered, I dozed off again. The next day we were detained longer than usual on parade, and that was the only effect upon us of the escape which, we found out later, had been successful. It is interesting to compare the result of this escape with what would have happened in my former camp IIIE, where the treatment was quite harsh. The following day, while the escapees were still at large, our biggest tunnel yet constructed was discovered when it was barely a few yards from the perimeter fence.

By this time it seemed to us that if ever a person escaped from this place it would be by an original and unexpected method. Tunnel digging seemed definitely to be out of the question now for we had decided that Jerry possessed some means of determining the whys and wherefores of our tunnelling systems. Despite this we had commenced a tunnel in our barrack, moulded on the lines of our IIIE effort, and the lads spared no pains on its construction. It progressed very slowly and caused the barracks in general no end of trouble. We were subjected to thorough searches by the 'moles' (German anti-escape squad, distinguished by dark blue overalls, and always to be seen digging), and at night they could be seen prowling around the barrack with their dogs in the hope of overhearing some chance remark which would give them a clue on which to work. They were obviously suspicious but had not been able to discover the exact position of the tunnel and it seemed that in some way we had outwitted them and their machine.

On the day following the discovery of the large tunnel, the Germans commenced the prison roster for the IIIE escapees who had all been sentenced to two weeks solitary in the cooler. Of the 51 of us who were recaptured not one had yet served his full sentence and we had thought that possibly they might forget and overlook the past — but no such luck. To start the ball rolling Jock and Breck served a 14-day term in solitary confinement. When released they gave us a description of the conditions of the cells and it was such a glowing account, contrasting so strongly with the IIIE cooler, that I began even to look forward to my sojourn there as a quiet change and a splendid opportunity for some much-needed study.

On 6 July we heard that General Rommel had been driven back in Africa and things began to look better in that theatre of war. Also on this day I received my first cigarette parcel, which brought our combine total to 25,000 received since 23 May. Six thousand Red Cross food parcels also arrived, causing much elation and barely had we got well into them when a further batch of 10,000 came, together with some clothing. As food rep I was being overwhelmed with work, but I didn't mind as it was a pleasant task. The store by now was bulging with food, the floor space being hopelessly inadequate for a camp of 2500; in fact, an overflow of parcels had to be stored in an adjoining barrack to relieve the congestion. Of course we were not alarmed at this — on the contrary we welcomed the thought that there might be so many parcels that the construction of a reserve store would be necessary. But I doubted whether it ever would as our supply was too irregular. We lived from day to day, never knowing whether the following week would see us hungry or satisfied.

Alexander McBride Kerr, aged 4, 1925

Alex, aged 10, 1931

Scots Wha Hae, aged 12, 1933

At home with Mum and Dad, aged 13, 1934

Wests Baseball Team, (centre row — Tom Nisbet, Alex), The Esplanade, Perth WA, 1937

16th Battalion Cameron Highlanders, (Alex - front row left; Bret Langridge - front row right; Frank Sublet - back row 2nd right), 1938

Sergeant in the Cameron Highlanders, 1939

First Inductees Empire Air Training Scheme (Alex — front 2nd left; Selwyn — front 2nd right), Perth, 27 April 1940

Five new recruits (Alex, centre), Somers, Victoria, 1940

Tiger Moth — my first love, Newcastle, 1940

One Course embarking for Canada (Selwyn and Alex, centre), Sydney, 1940

Ken, Sel and Alex on the Awatea, Honolulu, 1940

Fighter Training, North American Harvards, Ottawa, 1940

The Four Mascoteers, (left to right — Monty, Alex, Ken, Sel), Ottawa, 1940

One Course Pilots' Graduation, Ottawa, December, 1940

Above: Oberleutnant Eckart-Wilhelm von Bonin seen from the radio operator's position during preparations for take-off.
Left: Oberleutnant von Bonin (right) discusses a mission with his crew. He flew with II./NJG 1 from 1941, and was appointed commander of that Gruppe in 1943.
Below: Oberleutnant von Bonin 'bagged' this Wellington of 115 Squadron, RAF, which landed without further damage at Bonin's base.

*The man who shot me down.
in May 1941*

Above - Eckart-Wilhelm von Bonin and his crew
Below - Fire Damage to the port side of the Wellington that he bagged, 11 May 1941

prayer before I kicked the bucket. But I had never been a great church_____ that out when I attempted the Lord's Prayer, for there were some lines _____ could not remember. However I finished my prayer as best I could a_____ by the peculiar type of pain I was experiencing and not seeing any ad_____ dragging it on, I tried to end my rather unexciting life. This I attem_____ expedient of holding my breath. Fortunately however, for the compl_____ and sundry other reasons, I was unsuccessful, and after the tr_____ it up. I was still breathing heavily when the ambulance skidded _____ gravel drive outside a lonely hospital near the Danish border.

Dawn was just breaking and there was an invigorating a_____ as the sun slowly peeped his glowing orb over the distant hills. I _____ to appreciate this, however, as I was carried to the operating theatre_____ leave me, for a while, submitting reluctantly to the sickly- some_____ was gently placed over my face.

War diary extract   trip by ambulance to hospital, 1941

Professor René Simon (centre) with fellow prisoners, 1941

Prisoner of War Nº 182

THIS BOOK BELONGS TO

ALEXANDER KERR.
AUS. 406012.
Royal Australian Air Force.
1940 — 194 .

Y.M.C.A.

A Wartime Log - gift from YMCA Switzerland, 1941

Stalag IIIE - Anzacs all dressed up (back row - Alex far right, Herb 2nd from right), 1942

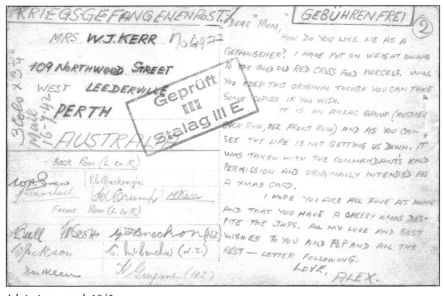

A kriegie postcard, 1942

Stalag Luft III (Alex standing 4th left), 1942

'Harmony Park', Stalag Luft III (Alex - 2nd right), 1943

'Girls Girls Girls', Stalag Luft III (Alex - kneeling front 2nd right), 1943

The Australian Test Team Stalag Luft VI, by Cal Younger, 1943

UNIVERSITY OF OXFORD

THIS IS TO CERTIFY that

Sgt. A. M. Kerr

a Prisoner of War, was examined at

Stalag Luft VI (357)

in November 1944 *under the authority of the University, in*
Principles of Economics   Industrial Organization*
Money and Banking   International Economics
and that the Examiners have reported that his work was of the
quality normally required for University Honours.
    * With Distinction.

UNIVERSITY REGISTRY
OXFORD
1st June 1945.

Assistant Registrar

Oxford University certificate, 1944

JULY 21, 1945

BEHIND THE WIRE
By Cal Younger

ECONOMICS
FRENCH
ENGLISH
HIST
GEOGR

W/O Alex Kerr, from West Perth, was shot
down over Hamburg in May, 1941. Badly
wounded, he was thrown out of the stricken
machine by members of his crew. Alex was
on number 1 course pilots and trained in
Canada, arriving in England at Xmas, 1940.
He was a newspaper man in civil life and
is at present completing a degree in Economics
for which he worked determinedly in Germany

Cartoon by Cal Younger

Back in Blighty - Brighton, England (left to right - Bill Legg, Herb Crump, Alex, Roger Dee), 1945

A new life - marriage to Joan Langridge, Perth, August 1947

Germany. Our crew (except me) meet with our nemesis (left to right - Bill Legg, Dave Fraser, Geoff Hogg, Eckart von Bonin), 10 May 1991

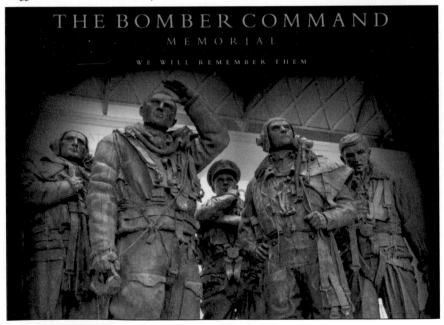

Memorial to Bomber Command, Green Park, London, 2012

Runnymede Memorial, England - for allied airmen who died in WW II with no known grave; a special place to remember my best friend Bob Blair, 2012

Alex at home with Jalaga (© *The West Australian*)

Chapter 19

About this time Freddie Woods received an unpleasant shock while walking around the compound one evening. He had been kicking a football in front of him as he strolled beside the warning fence, beyond which it was dangerous to venture. He took good care to avoid the fence and as he approached the sports field he dribbled the ball towards the posts with the intention of shooting for goal. He had just kicked the ball when a shot rang out from the watch tower behind him and a bullet kicked up the dust 10 feet to his right. He turned with rapidly mounting pulse and saw the guard with his rifle to his shoulder. He did not wait to see why the guard had fired; in a few seconds he was in the nearest hut.

Two days later Rocky Trites was by our window, attempting to attract the attention of Herb Crump, who was doing his sentence in gaol, the cells of which stood 200 yards away, separated from us by a barbed wire fence. Rocky had just succeeded in catching Herb's eye through the window when he heard the metallic click of a rifle bolt and turned to the searchlight tower which was about 20 yards away. The guard had cocked his rifle and was just in the act of raising it to his shoulder. Seeing the muzzle rising in line with his body Rocky pivoted on his heel and sprang for the door of the barrack. As his heel struck the step the shot rang out with alarming suddenness and a little green tomato in the vegetable garden fell silently to the ground. Rocky sat down and wiped the perspiration from his brow. These incidents every now and then reminded us that life was somewhat precarious and we had to be extra careful in observing the camp rules.

Sometime after this a new scheme was introduced whereby we were allowed to visit the latrines and wash-houses after dusk. Unfortunately the guards had not been acquainted with the new system with the result that one of our men came within an ace of losing his life. He had strolled out to the latrine in the fading dusk after the former lock-up time and had been spotted by a postern in a nearby tower, who had immediately trained his searchlight upon the latrine. This attracted the attention of another guard, who also brought round his searchlight beam. Thus they held the lad a prisoner in the latrine, which happened to be the one adjacent to our barrack.

'What's happening?' said Rocky. 'I thought the curfew had been cut out.'

'Yeah it has,' said Jock, 'but the guards are acting as though it hasn't. That poor bugger in the latrine is not game to come out because the guards have their searchlights trained on him.'

Eventually I got tired of watching and went back to our office. Hardly had I reached it when a shot split the silent night with a deafening report. A second shot sounded close on the first and as the echo died away we waited silently for the third. None came, however, and gradually the chatter began again in the room. Later we got the story from an eye witness. The lad in the latrine had finally decided to attempt the return to his barrack and stepped from the shadow of the door. He was instantly greeted by a shot which got him in the elbow. Needless to say, by the time the guard got in a second shot the prisoner was no longer there. He was back in the latrine, having taken the skin off his other elbow in his headlong dive for shelter. Shortly afterwards along came some 'moles' to take him to the cooler where he spent the remainder of the night. The next day, having been released with an apology — for it was all a gross mistake — he celebrated his 21st birthday. That party very nearly fell through.

These three cases of shootings are an illustration of the tendency of the posterns to be trigger happy. The slightest action which could be interpreted as suspicious — and in some cases even the most innocent of movements — resulted in a shot being fired which, though it may not have endangered the life of the person fired at, may at least have injured some other person in the line of fire.

On 24 July my turn in the cooler came and I strode over with my blankets, toilet articles, some carefully concealed cigarettes and several books. I intended to do some intensive study in several subjects and by the end of the 14 days my brain was really fatigued; apart from two hours' exercise each day, I spent the whole time reading and writing. The peace and quiet of the prison was a godsend and it enabled me to get through a lot of work.

On 1 August, while I was still in the cooler, an event of enormous importance to us took place. The first truckload of new potatoes arrived in the camp. Our rations had become particularly lean, the main staple being soft and deteriorating swede turnips and practically rotten potatoes, so we had been looking forward to receiving new springtime vegetables. Coincidentally with this good news came some bad news; we were to have our mail stopped. The Germans complained that German families were not receiving enough mail from German prisoners in Canada and stated that until the incoming mail improved, our own would be withheld. A notice was posted by the commandant stating that we would receive four letters per month and would be permitted to write one letter and one card per month. A special clause was inserted referring to Stalag XXA stating that until the Australian Government cooperated to a greater degree the Australian prisoners would neither receive nor be permitted to write any mail at all. It was not long, however, before this edict seemed to fade into memory and our mail began to assume some semblance of regularity once again.

On 7 August my sojourn in the cooler ended and I came out to make way for Ivan Quinn and Ken Stalder, both from my combine. The pleasing aspect of a sentence in the clink, apart from the opportunity for uninterrupted study, is that one's Red Cross parcels mounted up, as they are forbidden in the cells as a punishment and as soon as a man comes out he draws whatever he has missed. In this way our combines were constantly being supplied with extra parcels at the expense of whoever happened to be in the cooler on German rations.

CHAPTER 20
SPORTS AND ESCAPES, 1942

A note came over from the officers' compound on 6 August 1942 stating that the group captain (senior allied officer) hoped for a day of prayer on the 9th, to coincide as nearly as possible with that which was being held in England. An outdoor service was arranged and on that morning, which had dawned a fine day, the chaplain, accompanied by the group captain and several officers came across to conduct it. We paraded 1700 strong and the service, which was impressive and strongly reminiscent of Anzac Day gatherings in Australia, lasted an hour during which we stood bareheaded in the sun. The officers then returned under guard to their compound.

On Friday 14 August we held our compound sports, an event to which we had been looking forward with pleasure for some time. The prisoners who had volunteered as sports administrators had worked for some days on preparing the venues for the events and everything was in top condition. It was a fine day and the events went off well. In the track events we had the 100, 200, 400, 800 and 1500 yards, several relays, and a walking race. The field events included the shot-put, discus, broad jump, high jump, tossing the caber and many novelty events. The whole afternoon was a great credit to the organisers. The times and distances were rather poor due to a variety of causes including the condition of the track and the poor diet of a POW.

The following Monday the officers sent over a team from their compound to challenge us. The weather was again fine and the tracks had been maintained in good condition so we all looked forward to a good battle. The sergeants commenced well, holding a steady lead for the first half of the events and putting everyone in a good humour at the interval.

Chapter 20

After tea, however, the officers gradually made up ground until it became a matter of half a point difference in 90 points. The atmosphere became tense as the lead then alternated with each successive race.

When the final race was due to start the officers were leading by six points and the issue was still in doubt. It was a long race and the excitement mounted as the runners entered the final straight. A great shout of triumph went up when our first two representatives crossed the line, closely followed by an officer, giving us the victory by one point with a total of 131 to the officers' 130. The closeness of the struggle is evident from the final score and of course the day was a complete success. A real racetrack atmosphere prevailed, coloured by the strains of the stalag dance band which played from a sheltered stand, and the arresting voice of an enterprising bookmaker who conducted his business with cigarettes, giving good odds on all races. At the close of the meeting the group captain presented prizes won on both days and concluded with a speech thanking the German commandant for allowing the officers to come across.

A long spell of hot weather set in after this and many sports were introduced. Some softball equipment had arrived for one of the boys and although it was not a large quantity it provided the means of forming a small league which ran for a month or so until the balls became worn out and useless. Basketball, soccer, rugby and field hockey also came into full swing and a happy summer holiday atmosphere prevailed.

We strolled onto parade at the usual hour on the evening of 21 August and stood around waiting for the German officer to put in an appearance. Another thunderstorm was threatening and dark clouds tinged with a dull metallic red towered above the eastern horizon in silent rolls. Small, low black patches of cloud, couriers for the brewing storm, raced swiftly across the sky from east to west into the dying sun. The storm was long overdue; the hot spell had lasted more than a fortnight which, from our observations since we had been here, we regarded as a period of unprecedented length. The feeble half-moon was vainly trying to push its way through the heavy bank of angry clouds which was moving on quickly; it succeeded merely in peeping through now and again, only to be lost a second later.

125

SHOT DOWN

The hauptmann (captain) finished checking the parade and stood in the centre of the parade ground surrounded by his aides talking with Dixie Dean, our compound captain. Time began to drag and the boys showed signs of restlessness. The oppressive pre-storm atmosphere, the hauptmann's refusal to allow smoking, the constant standing in one position with the prospect of remaining there for many more minutes, all combined to give the parade an air of impatience, of tense waiting. Of course, we all — or most of us — knew the cause of the delay. Someone had escaped! Someone had got away from this camp which was regarded as escape-proof. Most of us already knew of the break, which had occurred the previous day, and the confusion and delay on parade which followed the German's discovery that one of their birds had flown, we regarded as the inevitable result.

So out came cigarettes, furtively at first and then openly. Someone in the ranks began a small fire on the parade ground and in the fading dusk it flared up. Regardless of the guards, the boys began an Indian war dance around it and the ranks spread out as they circled the fire emitting weird yells with the hauptmann staring on in hatchet-faced silence. It was difficult to determine whether he was dumb with rage or speechless with amazement as he stood glaring at them for a few minutes without speaking.

Finally he gave the order for which we were all waiting, to our man of confidence, Dixie Dean. Dixie bade the boys extinguish the fire. This was obeyed and a hush fell on the parade as Dixie stepped forward to make an announcement. He said but a few words informing us of what we had already guessed — that someone had escaped. A great burst of cheering broke out and continued for more than a minute, while the hauptmann and his non-commissioned satellites and the guards stood looking on in stony silence. After that we wandered back to our barracks in the dark, chatting and laughing.

A few mornings later, 22 August, Hauptmann Jacob announced to us that an English force had landed in France and had been repulsed. This rather uncompromising and brief statement was the first we knew of the disastrous Dieppe raid by a Canadian force. Eventually we got most of the details from the German authorities and a week or so later we were shown a German newsreel giving a graphic presentation of the action seen from the town of Dieppe itself. Some 1500 prisoners, mostly Canadians, were taken and sent to Stalag VIIIB, a well-known army camp which contained a lot of Australian Army prisoners. The Germans claimed 112 Allied aircraft shot down. The whole action lasted barely 12 hours. Numerous ships and tanks were seized and the attacking party withdrew towards evening. It was a decisive defeat for the Allies. After a few days, the excitement caused by the incident died down and life became normal again.

On 23 August our first softball game in the newly formed league took place and it swung into its first season with the support of all the Canadians. It had for critics a considerable number of sarcastic Englishmen who declaimed a sport which seemed to rely mainly for its support on talking. At the end of the season, however, it became a common and somewhat amusing sight to see some of the very 'English' Englishmen trying their hand — or rather their voice at 'rooting' for their favourite team.

Sports played a predominant part in our stalag life at this period of fine weather and on 31 August began a series of boxing contests. They were held in a ring constructed on trestles in the open. The contest continued for three days and provided some interesting bouts. Lieutenant Commander Buckley came over from the officers' compound to referee the finals, which drew a large attendance and brought to light some good boxers, particularly among the Poles.

About this time I received news that Bill, who had now been in the Sagan Lazarette (hospital) for some months, was to undergo another operation which, if successful, would put him on his feet, cured and as sound as could be hoped for. A French surgeon of some repute was to operate and he was confident of success. Several days later we heard that the operation itself was a success but that during the night complications had set in and he was now in a critical condition. As far as I can gather he almost died that night, but he recovered slowly and eventually found himself in a similar condition to before. On 21 October he was passed by the Swiss Repatriation Board for repatriation to England.

SHOT DOWN

On 3 September we held our first arts and crafts exhibition, which was a great success bringing, as it did, before the eyes of the rest of the camp the astounding results of the efforts of a small minority. The art section comprised many paintings of still life and some good portraits contributed by a few capable artists. The crafts section, a truly amazing display of badges, needlework and a variety of models, displayed a depth of imagination, ingenuity and perseverance, hard to credit. Some of the exhibits were beautifully finished and there was a working model of a small steam engine which had been used to propel a raft made from jam tins across the fire pond. When one considers the lack of conventional tools and materials the effort becomes truly amazing and enough praise cannot be given to the creators of those models.

About this time I struck up a friendship with Tony Johnston, a tall air force sergeant-pilot who had recently come into the camp. At least that is who the Germans knew him as. In fact he was a Frenchman who had changed identities with an air force sergeant-pilot by the name of Tony Johnston who wanted to escape. Tony spoke English and I spoke French. We both wanted to improve our foreign language so we used to do a few circuits of the perimeter wire each evening. Tony spoke in English and I spoke in French and as we went we corrected each other.

Tony would say, 'Good morning, Alex. How are you today?' And I would counter with. 'Bonjour, Tony. Je vais bien merci.'

I would ask him if there was any interesting news today: 'Des nouvelles interressantes ce matin?'

'Rien de toute consequence,' he might reply; nothing of any consequence. And so our talk would go on about the weather, the war, anything.

After the war we continued our friendship by playing chess by post.

On 15 September F/Sgt AFP James, an Australian spitfire pilot, arrived. He had been badly burnt on the face. His reputation rapidly spread and we realised that here at last we had the prince of line-shooters to contend with. His tales of experiences in the Sino-Japanese war and the Spanish civil war, in addition to his adventures while going to and from the scenes of action, provided us with an unconscionable field for thought and our wonder was that he was merely a sergeant.

128

Chapter 20

'I joined the RAAF before the war,' he told me, 'and got to the rank of flight-lieutenant pretty quickly but we were stuck in Australia, away from all the excitement. So I finally decided to take a runner without telling anyone and I shot through to Spain where they accepted me as an experienced pilot. It didn't take me long to talk them into making me a major with the Spanish loyalists. On one occasion I mixed it with a German Stuka but neither of us got a hit. I could see that I was on the wrong side of that conflict and it wasn't long before I became interested in Claire Chennault's Flying Tigers in China and the faster aircraft they used. I eventually deserted the Spanish Air Force and made my way slowly up the coastal areas of the South China Sea, in Cambodia and Vietnam, to Southern China. The Chinese Air Force was not very strong or formidable and after about a year I had become a lieutenant-colonel. But the RAF and those beautiful spitfires they had were drawing me away from combat with the Japanese zeros and finally I left China and made my way to England. It wasn't easy and it took me quite a while.'

'When I applied to the RAF I wasn't game to reveal my previous service with the RAAF so I enrolled as an erk [aircraftman] and got my wings as a sergeant pilot. At last I was flying the best fighter in the air. I flew my spitfire for 25 sorties before an ME 109 shot me down. So here I am.'

His stories were so tall that only the truly gullible became convinced and soon most kriegies were laughing at him.

His notoriety in the camp subsided after a week or two and he fell into the rut of things with his organisations and schemes, some of which reflected credit upon him, others which evoked indignant protests from those whose toes he proposed to tread upon. He had a brilliant brain but was lacking perhaps in common sense. I thought to myself that as long as this didn't keep tripping him up he would go far with his analytical mind, his prodigious memory, his literary ability and his enraging cocksureness and self-confidence.

'Alfie', as he was known, was a man of many parts. He was so unpopular that he eventually had to enlist the protection of a bodyguard (one was Dave Fraser, my air gunner). Some prisoners thought he was selling secrets to the Germans. There was a great deal of uncertainty about his status because occasionally he was taken out of the compound by German guards to have morning tea with the camp commandant. The alternative theory, to which I subscribed and thus retained friendly relations with him, was that he was a member of British intelligence. As a third possibility he could merely have been one of the great con artists of all times!

Before we left Kirchain the Gestapo interrogator drew Jock Alexander aside and said, 'Flight sergeant, we know that you traded with some of our guards and that you obtained food and articles that you wanted. You are now going to Stalag Luft III and if you change your mind and decide to give us some of the information we want it's just a matter of letting the commandant know and he will get in touch with us in Berlin. You can send two informants and I will guarantee that they will be treated very well and returned in good shape.'

Jock nodded. 'I'll bear that in mind,' he said.

It was when we were safely ensconced in Stalag Luft III that we held a meeting one day and elected two representatives to take with them to Berlin a list of the Germans who had traded with us. Off they went, in due course, to Berlin where they spent two pleasant days as guests of the Gestapo. They were wined and dined and had quite an enjoyable time after handing over the list of names. The finale came several weeks later when we heard that the camp commandant had been sent to the Russian front, the camp administrative officer had received 10 years in gaol and the other guards on our list had each received gaol sentences.

In retrospect it is probable that most of us felt rather guilty about the result because only we knew that the names on the list were not the names of the Germans who traded with us but the names of the Germans who had maltreated us. Stalag IIIE was a camp in which violence had earlier been used and prisoners had been bashed by guards and subjected to harsh treatment ordered by the commandant. It was a strange sort of poetic justice which led to the main players in this drama paying with their liberty for what they did to us while those who were truly guilty of trading (most of whom we found rather friendly and helpful) went scot-free.

CHAPTER 21

SECOND CHRISTMAS IN PRISON, 1942

On 19 October our newly reconditioned theatre was opened with a long variety show as its premiere. The change was remarkable to say the least; the whole interior of the theatre was transformed and an illusion of striking reality created. The Germans cooperated by providing props and our own boys excelled themselves with the lighting and stage effects. The show which included a burlesque *Rigoletto* took us miles from Sagan and its barbed wire and held us there for two hours of music and laughter which, unfortunately, only served to make us feel more miserable when at the end of the show we were precipitated once more into the stark reality of our dimly lit huts.

At these times I found it interesting to reflect on the change of emotions which always seemed to be a side effect of the stage shows we had. For a few hours kriegies were lost in the emotions played out on the stage before them. For the most part they were watching comedy and excited by the theatre, laughing and joking. But it did not take more than a few minutes before they were drawn into self-reflection and contrasts and thoughts of their loved ones and their friends and this always brought with them thoughts about what they were doing and concerns about their safety. For instance, my brother was a flight-lieutenant commanding fast sea rescue boats in the Japanese theatre. It was hazardous work. So, in one day or a few hours one could go through the whole gamut of emotions with their inevitable effects on the psyche.

Armistice Day, 11 November, was observed with a service conducted by Captain Robinson, who came over from the officers' compound. On the same day the letter ban was raised. I received 42 in all —

enough to keep me happy for many days. Whenever I received batches of mail in large quantities I felt restless for a few days, but it eventually wore off.

On 16 November, according to German radio, the Axis powers evacuated Tobruk and it seemed that our armies were advancing again. The news we got after this was veiled in the usual nebulous OKW (German High Command) statements, but we could see that our armies were marching onwards until, at the moment of writing, the enemy had but a small line of coast from Tripoli to Tunis. It seemed as if, with a stroke of luck, the British Government may be able to give Africa to the Allied armies as a new year's gift.

On 21 November, Bill returned from hospital in Lamsdorf. I succeeded in seeing him the following day. He said, 'I hope I'm allowed to come over to your compound for Christmas. This, however, he could not do as his wound began to discharge once more and he was sent back to the French hospital in Sagan. November saw our first Amateur Dramatic Society production — *Meet Mrs Mandon* — written and produced by a POW. The acting was good and the play was well received.

Three days later we received news of the Toulon incident, again somewhat vague and twisted, from which we gathered that officers of the French Fleet had distinguished themselves and vindicated the previous slight to their honour which had been caused by their surrender in 1940. Many of their officers and men perished as they sank their ships, but they prevented the Germans from seizing their navy.

On 5 December we opened a keg of 'home-brew', a wine which we had made from dried raisins. It was simple to make and the ingredients readily obtainable from Red Cross parcels and the German cookhouse. The barrel was almost filled with water and dried raisins added. Sugar was stirred in with it and a little yeast added. In a matter of hours the brew began to work and from then onwards it was simply a matter of adding sugar whenever it began to taste sour. After 10 days the brew was strained through a singlet and the messy raisin slush discarded. The remaining brew was then returned to the barrel and sealed on the top with a large rock. On the following Saturday it was broached.

The brew emitted a soft hissing sound as the rock was carefully lifted. The effect of the liquor was not apparent at first but as the clock ticked over the tongues became loosened and the conversation became louder. The war situation was discussed at length and varying opinions on the date of the surrender, which was always a German surrender, were batted about. The respective attractions and detractions of the various countries represented in the room were thrust forward with increasing emotion and increasing vehemence and the respective merits of various kinds of sport were strongly debated until the participants became exhausted.

In our stomachs was the warm comforting glow, the memory of which had almost slipped into the dim mists of the forgotten past; in our eyes was the glassy stare, the sight of which we had hoped to see again someday; in our voices was that happy slur which warns one when to stop.

The news that we had opened our keg soon spread quickly, and before long we had many visitors pouring into our little room at the end of No. 39 Hut. Many were friends we never knew we possessed, all forming a seething, struggling, singing, happy mass of bodies swaying to and from the barrel. Needless to say the poor barrel could not stand much treatment like that and before long Suggy, shouting over the noisy hubbub, announced that we'd 'had it'.

''S bout time we shtopped!' shouted Suggy. 'Bloody keg's empty. Lesh try some of the other huts.' This caused us to seek our entertainment elsewhere so we did the rounds of the camp to all the other huts that had managed to make themselves some brew until we finally tumbled into bed tired but happy at midnight. Brek and Suggy sang us to sleep with 'I Wonder Who's Kissing Her Now'.

The effect soon wore off the next morning leaving us sober enough to go over to the officers' band show. We, the Red Cross reps of each hut, had received an invitation to go to the final performance of the officers' variety show. At 8.00 pm we were met by a dolmetscher (interpreter) who took us through the main gate up the path to the officers' compound. Wing Commander 'Friar' Tuck, the Spitfire ace, and Flying Officer Ogelvy, the Canadian officer who received his

Distinguished Flying Cross for shooting down a German bomber that had attacked Buckingham Palace, received us in the adjutant's office and shortly afterwards we made our way to the theatre where the show started at 8.30 pm. It was highly amusing and very enjoyable and was crowned by the appearance, at the end, of the Group Captain who made another of his well-known impromptu speeches and declared the show over.

It was on 17 December that our first ice hockey match took place. Of course most of the players were Canadians but the attendances showed the keen interest in the game which was displayed by the rest of the camp. Unfortunately the cold spell lasted for only a week or so and we did not get a good chance to learn the finer points of the game.

Nothing more of interest occurred until the eve of 24 December. The actual night itself did not compare with that of the previous year and the same carefree, defiant spirit of comradeship that existed at IIIE seemed to be lacking somewhat. No doubt this was due to some extent to the fact that here there were many camps combined and the fact that the prisoners had been incarcerated for another year. The impressions left on one's mind seem to be stronger and more vivid than before. The year just completed was, in almost all its aspects, a sorry one. After 12 months of depressing news, despite America coming into the conflict, the general spirit in the camp was low. The extra-optimistic kriegies who had expected the war to be over by now were hardest hit but even the 'realists', as they saw themselves, had not expected such a dismal year. Most of them entered the new year with more sober expectations for the future and justifiably so.

Fired to enthusiasm by the undoubted success of our previous effort we had laid down another brew, timed to mature nicely by Christmas Eve. It did. In addition to that, however, the Germans had sold us some beer which had arrived some days beforehand. We, in our little office, had succeeded in buying, for chocolate and cigarettes, enough portions of beer to enable us to install a whole barrel of beer in our room. At approximately seven o'clock the barrel was tapped and we all took our seats around the room, which had been decorated above and cleared for action below. The first glasses were tasted, the quality approved of and the work begun, conversation at first flowing in the desultory manner which was the prelude to a noisy drinking bout.

At the end of half an hour, however, the eyes, expressions and actions of everyone were quite normal. The conversation, instead of being more animated, was in fact somewhat subdued. At the end of an hour the awful truth stared us in the face. The beer was no good. Conversation had fallen to a minimum and no more sombre nor gloomy set of faces could have been found in any kriegie camp than that in our office at 8 o'clock that Christmas Eve. Stark sobriety stared us in the face!

It was a crisis of the greatest magnitude.

'What do you think, Jock?' I asked. 'Do we wait for Christmas Day or do we open our Christmas brew now?'

'Well, we have a group of thirsty drinkers here now and to prevent Christmas Eve from being a complete flop I think we should probably open the other keg.'

'Quinny and Suggy, what do you think?' I asked. They both agreed with Jock.

'Let's crack it open,' they said in unison.

Recourse was therefore had to the yellow raisin wine and within half an hour things began to pick up. By ten o'clock we were singing with many others (for home-brews by the dozen had appeared from nooks and crannies) in Barrack 51 where the dance band was dispensing music.

By eleven o'clock those of us who remained on our feet were searching for the others who had fallen by the wayside. By twelve o'clock we had found them again, in time to join on to the end of a terrific 'snake' which was wending its unsteady way from barrack to barrack led by Stan Paris, the local trumpet player. Most of the boys were back in the barracks by one o'clock (lock-up and lights outs) even though some did have to be assisted to bed. Things began to quieten down until even the after-dark chattering lapsed into a medley of contented snores. So much for Christmas 1942.

During this week, and through January, events out of the ordinary happened with such rapidity that it is possible only to tabulate them here. We had a variety show, *Bums on Broadway,* which was well accepted by the audiences, particularly as it marked the debut of our new female star 'Junior Booth', a blond whose only drawback was his big legs.

On the same evening, while most of the German officers and interpreters were at the show, Morris and Grimson made a masterful but short-lived getaway from the camp. Sometime after the German group had been let through the gate to attend the show, the two appeared at the gate in what appeared to be German officers' uniforms and demanded to be let out immediately. The guard was some distance from the gate on his guard beat and came running back to his post. Grimson so berated the guard (in flawless German) for being away from the gate that in a fluster he let them through without asking to see their passes. It was not until the party of officers came to go through the gate after the show that the guard discovered that he had two men extra. He wanted to arrest the last two attempting to go through the gate. Unfortunately the two escapees were apprehended on the Sagan railway station by an officer from the camp who happened to be travelling on leave and who recognised the two escapees from their previous escapades.

Some of the escapes were skilful exhibitions of ingenuity, intelligence and cool nerve. Grimson, who was reported finally to have met his death in Poland while working with the Polish underground to facilitate the passage of other escaped prisoners, was undoubtedly the master of them all. On his last escape from Stalag Luft III he dressed himself as a German unter-offizier (NCO) and equipped himself with a pair of headphones attached by wire to a little black box from which protruded a handle and two wires with crocodile clips.

At lunch, when the goons (German maintenance workers) left their equipment inside the compound and made off to the German mess hut for their meal, Grimson picked up a ladder, carried it to the nearest German sentry box, propped it against the wire and climbed up the ladder. He took the wires and clipped them to the top of the barbed wire fence, at the same time explaining in perfect German to the interested postern in the nearby guard box that he was testing for hidden electronic equipment. He then put the earphones on his head, twirled the handle of the little black box and listened intently.

Chapter 21

After doing this two or three times, he climbed down the ladder still on the inside of the camp and strolled over to the other nearby guard box where he repeated the procedure. Finally at the end of about 15 minutes he made his way to the central part in between the two guard boxes, climbed up the ladder, carried out his tests, shouted to the guards that he was lazy and couldn't be bothered going back down and through the gate then pulled the ladder up and placed it on the outside. He then climbed down the ladder, carefully placed his equipment on the ground beside the ladder, shouted to the guards that he was going to lunch and that he wanted them to make sure that no-one took his equipment and walked off, never to be seen again.

This was but one of the many efforts supported by the escape committee and by prisoners in the camp who performed absolutely amazing feats in transforming pieces of rag, silver paper, string, rubber, wood, plastic and anything else available into German uniforms, current official German passes, civilian clothes, attaché cases and almost anything one could turn one's mind to. Many of the successful escapes were in no small measure due to the invaluable artistry and skill of others who stayed behind. These were the unsung heroes of the prison camps.

On the first day of the new year, 1943, Barrack 4 was thoroughly searched and Bristow taken away to the cooler. McKenzie and Akehurst were already there awaiting a court martial for charges of sabotage, and striking a German.

Three days later the Entertainments Committee presented our Christmas pantomime *Aladdin*, somewhat belated but nevertheless welcome and well accepted. It was voted the best entertainment yet and was notable for the lavish scenery and stage sets. As we encored the artists I could not help contrasting the happy spirit in the hall with the probable state of affairs in Stalag VIIIB where the prisoners were still chained. They must have suffered a great deal and no doubt our hard times at IIIE, which was, as far as we could see, the worst RAF camp at that time, must seem easy when compared with the conditions now existing at Lamsdorf.

CHAPTER 22
TURN OF THE TIDE, 1943

On 22 January I was having my constitutional walk when I was surprised to see Bill walking through the gate. 'Hey, Bill!' I called. 'What a surprise! Good to see you again. What's happened? Have they discharged you from hospital?'

'Well, I'm not sure actually,' replied Bill. 'I think the idea is for me to go to the French hospital regularly, say every second day, to have my dressings changed but I think they have decided that I don't need to be there full-time, occupying a bed. So it looks as though I'll be here for a while.' He told me that the doctors seemed to think that in all probability he would remain a patient there for some time. They still talked of the chances of him being repatriated.

I was glad to see him and to note that despite the trying times he had been through he was still as bright as ever and looking fitter than he had been for some time.

About this time the camp was feeling very optimistic as the German newspapers themselves were spreading a shadow of gloom upon the people of Germany. Veiled hints and admissions of military reversals led us to believe that the possibility of the war ending in 1943 was by no means remote provided, of course, that the Allies invaded in the spring.

The following article, illustrating the trend of the national newspapers, appeared in the *Volkischer Beobachter*, 14.1.43:

There is, in war, no glorious undertaking that is accomplished without endless effort, trouble and need. When the weakness of the physical and spiritual man is ready to give up, only a great force of will can lead to the goal which proclaims itself in an endurance astonishing to the world and to the world to follow. — Clausewitz.

This quotation from one of Germany's prominent philosophers when coupled with the fall of Stalingrad, a crushing blow to German military might, sounded to our minds like a significant note and marked a turning point in the policy of German newspapers, if not the German High Command itself.

By 25 January a situation which was to my mind amusing and at the same time worrying was soon the main focus of all idle chatter. We had a pair of lovers in the hut. Nothing could be proved, and having neither the interest nor the inclination to investigate myself, I accepted the more or less circumstantial evidence offered by the scandalmongers of the hut.

I was disinclined to believe the tales I heard, but just supposing that the assertions were true it set one's mind working along strange lines. When the full facts were considered and if due credence was given to tales from other camps, especially the army ones, it did seem strange that more cases of either actual or suspected homosexuality had not been disclosed. Some weeks later the enamoured pair had drifted apart due to what the wits of the hut called a 'lovers' quarrel', but their place had been taken by another two.

And talking of scandal brings me to another aspect of our little community here. Its likeness to the social community of a small town was becoming increasingly apparent. We had our political intrigues generated by the numerous committees that had been formed since our installation. The main obsession of the kriegie seems to be a mania for forming committees and rosters. And so, after nine months, we had an Entertainment Committee with its various sub-branches (Variety, Revue, Drama, Musical); the Debating Society with its sub-branch, the Literary Club; the Education Committee with its group of lecturers; several Language Societies and Social Discussion Groups; Scientific Discussion Groups; the Central Sports Committee with its many sub-branches; the Church Committee and the Toc H Committee; and many others all clamouring for space and time in the few small rooms set aside for that purpose.

Resultant from this we had an ever-increasing rivalry and competition which often led to petty quarrelling and bickering between the editors whose opinions on various events often differed widely. We now had three newspapers: one of them, the daily, taking a rather conservative outlook on most things; another, a weekly, revealing the liberal leanings of its progressive editor; and the third, a sports paper, representing but one part of the camp's activities and at the same time relieving the other two of a good deal of work.

Our small town scandal emanated from the members of the various committees, particularly the entertainment committee. Some of the leading players in our stage shows, taking the roles of males and females, became the subject of idle rumour and gossip suggesting that they had developed an unhealthy affection for one another off the stage. The flame of talk was either quenched or fanned into lesser or greater proportions by one of the newspapers.

On 5 February a band show was staged. Jack Fulkerson, Ron Charlesworth and I had been working up some vocal trio numbers and we made our first appearance with Ron Bush's 14-piece dance band. The big band had a full complement of instruments and they made good music. We also had hired evening suits and dinner jackets from Berlin and the whole show had quite a professional air to it. It was great fun and we thoroughly enjoyed ourselves.

The show was instrumental in my seeing an old school pal of mine, Geoff Cornish, who had left Perth shortly before the war to join the RAAF on the Short Service Commission scheme and had been shot down a month before me. It was during the interval of a matinee we gave for the officers that I had the chance of exchanging a few words with him. He told me that he was permitted to work in the German sick bay as he had planned to take a medical degree after the war. (To complete the record, I saw him several times after the war. He became a very successful and much-loved cardiac specialist in Queensland until his death.)

Around this time one of our fellows, McAllister by name, provided the camp with a mild diversion and a subject for discussion when, on 21 February, he calmly stepped over the warning wire and walked up to the main wire seemingly oblivious to the rifle bullets that were flying around him. He eventually raised his hands and the guards ceased firing. He was ultimately sent to hospital where he remained under observation for a considerable time. This was the first case of its kind that we had had since June last year when one of our fellows had attempted, unsuccessfully, to cut his throat. Four days later two fellows from his hut attempted to escape, but all they got for their pains was a mauling by one of the German police dogs, of which there were quite a few here.

Two days after this two more chaps, this time from the far end of the compound, attempted to escape by crawling to the fence on an overcast night. They were seen, however, and several machine gun bursts sent a hail of lead flying around the huts. One of the chaps had crouched behind a brick incinerator where he was reasonably safe, but the other lad was hit in several places and seriously wounded. He was carried off to hospital and died several weeks later.

After this period of escape-mania had subsided somewhat, the camp became comparatively quiet and there was nothing to report but theatrical productions and sporting events.

On 10 March I registered with the London University for the intermediate examination of the B.Sc. (Econ.), which meant further intensive study if I wished to complete the syllabus by November. Shortly afterwards I relinquished my position as Red Cross food representative, in order to achieve this end. On 8 April I was initiated into the Toc H group after a three-month probation. My only regret was that, owing to pressure of work, I could not give much time to their activities.

On 10 April Stephenson, an Aussie, returned from Schubin, whither he had gone as a batman the previous year. He had returned disappointed that Schubin did not appear to have any better chance for escape than Luft 3. He had news for me of some of my pals who had been with me in Canada.

'I ran into a couple of Aussies at Schubin,' he said. 'Alan McSweyn and Jock McKechnie. Apparently they were on No. 1 course with you. They were shot down after you. Both in good shape. They send their regards.'

They had arrived in Sagan at the same time as Stephenson and were over in the officers' compound. (McSweyn escaped a year later and flew back to Australia with the award of the Military Cross.) Steve also told us of the 'breaks' from Schubin, the largest of which had taken place several days before they left to come here. There had been three casualties, all of them Germans! The Gestapo panicked, of course, with plenty of curses floating around. One German officer complained to one of the prisoners: 'From the fuss the Gestapo are making you would think I had helped you to build the bloody tunnel.'

On the same day a new Aussie padre came to the camp and I was agreeably surprised to find that he was from Subiaco, the district adjoining that in which I had lived all my life. More than that, he had been with my old Battalion at Crete and could give me news of many of my former friends.

Sometime previous to this, one of the prisoners had stolen a German cap and as a result had brought down upon our heads the wrath of the Germans, which manifested itself in a number of restrictions. Among these was the closing of the theatre and the imposition of an extra parade each day. These restrictions were removed on 8 May and the theatre reopened to the tune of Somerset Maugham's *Home and Beauty*.

Good Friday and my birthday fell on 23 April; I just lazed in the sun all day and did no study for three days. I just soaked up the sun and thought of home and wondered what everyone was doing and where they were. I felt that the previous year had been mostly a waste of time and a miserable year in which hardly anything seemed to go right. I hoped that we wouldn't have another year like that. It didn't seem likely. The Americans were now operating with their powerful navy in the Pacific and engaging the Japanese armies in China and the Indo-Chinese peninsular, and the British and other allied forces were now having some successes in the Middle East. The bombing of Germany was having a formidable toll on the Axis industrial production and all in all the tide seemed to be turning. Thank heavens for the BBC news I thought. At least helps to keep our spirits up.

It was rather a crammed weekend for me, as Sunday was both Easter Day and Anzac Day, and on the intervening Saturday I played in a challenge softball match. The emotions on my birthday reminded me of my notable 21st birthday when Cal, the Canadian who was shot when recaptured with Suggy after our escape, came up to me in Stalag IIIE on the morning of 23 April 1942 with an egg.

Since the softball season had started, I and another Aussie, Jack Connelly, had noticed a growing interest in the game among the

Aussies. We therefore decided to form an Aussie team, believing that previous cricket experience would stand the boys in good stead. We were right. In fact the results were far better than we had expected. The boys responded to our coaching efforts and soon we found ourselves with two Australian teams and a long waiting list should we decide to form another.

The first Aussie team batted its way through the International League, losing only one match and that to the second Aussie team.

This eventually led to a reaction among the Canadians who regarded it as their game. 'Hey, Alex,' said Blackie, the captain of the Canadian team, 'if you think you're so good how about trying yourself against a good team? You've beaten another Aussie team and teams from other countries but that's no great feat. Wait till you take on an experienced Canadian team. Let's arrange a match between the Aussies and my first division Canadian team.'

Of course I could not let a challenge like that go unheeded so I snapped him up and arranged a match for Easter Sunday, placing a side wager of 1000 cigarettes on the result. I did not expect that we would win but I thought that at least we could show them that we could play their game almost as well as they. Experience would be, of course, the telling factor as our chaps had been only a month at the game.

It attracted the largest crowd for some time and ended in an exciting win 12–10 for the Canucks. It was played in a good spirit and was anybody's game to the last. It proved our point that we considered ourselves capable, now, of fielding a team worthy of a place in the National League. This was later arranged.

On 11 May it was my second anniversary of being shot down and my first anniversary of the escape from Kirchain. I celebrated by sleeping in the sun all day. On the same day the repatriation board visited the hospital and passed for repatriation, among others, Bill Legg and Ginger Hughes, who were both in hospital with me in Schleswig.

I was glad to see that at last these two, having endured pain and discomfort for months on end and false alarms about repatriation, were finally being sent home. I was happy for them. I was envious, of course, but my chest wound was finally healed and I was quite sure that there was now no reason why I should be repatriated so I was resigned to remaining a prisoner unless I could escape.

Two days later, when the officers came over to our compound for a variety show I had the chance of seeing Alan McSweyn, Clive Hall and Jock McKechnie all from No. 1 intake, Empire Air Training Scheme. We exchanged news of all our mutual friends particularly those whom we had made in Canada.

There were now at least six prisoners from our No. 1 intake of pilots and there was news of many more having already been killed in action. At the end of the war only 12 of the original 40 remained alive and of them 9 were prisoners. The sad statistics clearly told a grim story — to remain alive one had best get shot down and survive the experience.

Reflecting on these grim statistics I penned my third poem:

Sons of Perth

O lovely city, hope of many souls,
Whose memory oft doth soothe the throbbing heart,
How many of thy sons will not return,
Those lads who, daring death, did so depart.

Born in thy womb, a part of thee e'en now,
In a mortal struggle greatest of the earth,
They bloodied fell — not theirs to feel again,
The comfort thou hast tendered from their birth.

Thy voice is quiet now, the hush of death;
Has settled o'er thy bosom with a blow,
There are already some whose laugh is still,
And some, still laughing now, who soon will go.

Whate'er the outcome be of all this strife,
Their memory ever cherished shall we hold,
Though they no longer share with us this life,
The thoughts we hold of them are edged with gold.

CHAPTER 23
STALAG LUFT VI: HEYDEKRUG, EAST PRUSSIA, 1943

The rumours which had been prevalent for more than a month seemed to bear more weight and were tainted with the timbre of authority. It became definite on 1 June that we would soon be moving to Konigsberg in North Prussia. The Americans and the Poles, first to move, were sent to Barth. It left a big gap in the ranks of the softball players and apart from that the rather stimulating effect of their unmistakable accent was lost to the camp. A few days later our last musical show, before the break-up of the camp, was acclaimed the best show yet.

By 16 June we were preparing for our move and had most of our packing finished a day or two before the time scheduled for our departure. Some of the groups had already gone and the camp was beginning to take on the aspect of one of Goldsmith's deserted villages. Our turn came on 18 June and we were entrained in the early afternoon after a cursory search in the vorlager. We found to our pleasure that we were not packed so tightly as is usually the case on a journey of this type and we travelled in third-class coaches instead of cattle trucks, our first experience of this luxury.

The journey provided a more than welcome diversion in our kriegie life and we took full advantage of it. One fact which impressed itself on my mind was the effect which this life was having upon us with regard to that delightful subject, 'woman'. Whenever the train chanced to stop at a station there would follow a scramble for best place at the window. Men who had not seen or spoken to a girl for two, three years or more almost fought for the opportunity to gaze through the sealed window at the German lasses. I shuddered to think of what would happen to the girls when the first boatload of returned prisoners landed on England's shores.

We found on our arrival that our new camp on the shores of the Baltic was quite large, as we had expected, but nowhere near completion. It was divided into several compounds of 2000 capacity each. The Germans were still busy equipping our compound, which was the first to be occupied. This meant that the camp authorities would not be anywhere near prepared, for some time to come, to accept the many RAF prisoners from Lamsdorf. This was unfortunate because I felt sure that I must know some of the RAAF prisoners there of whom, I heard, there were about 200, mostly shot down in the Middle East.

As for the camp itself, we received with mixed feelings the news that a communal system of messing had been instituted, but realised that with the absence of adequate stoves in the hut it was the only workable scheme. The lighting in the huts was very poor and I realised that unless conditions were improved we would have very little opportunity for study during the long winter nights. Also I soon came to learn that in this part of the country there is no respect for seasons. In mid-summer it rains as blithely as in mid-winter it snowed. I protested bitterly against this system.

On 16 July the compound turned out en masse to see the first test between England and Australia and we had a perfect day for it. Because we had only 69 Aussies to pick from and there were 1700 Englishmen in the camp it was expected that Australia would not have much of a show, but we were determined to beat the Poms. We had quite a good line-up and I felt sure that we would put up a better show than was expected of us.

The English captain, Burbridge, won the toss and sent us in to bat. It was a very tricky wicket, a bowler's paradise, and we were all out before lunch for 88 with England on 2 for 20. After lunch England went on to make 114 altogether, which left us with quite a few runs to get in order to enable us to have any chance at all of winning. We did slightly better this time and ran up 99 by tea-time, leaving England a target of 74 for a win. Owing to excellent bowling by John Connelly and Frank Raymond, they were all out for 70 and we carried off the first test by three runs. Little did we ever think that over a year later another England–Australia test match would be fought to a close finish with Australia once again winning by three runs.

On 19 July I made my debut in the Stalag Debating Society when, with John Connelly, I supported the motion that 'This house would favour post-war compulsory labour service'. The motion, which as far as we were concerned consisted mainly of supporting and extending the Beveridge Plan, was carried by 66 votes to 15.

On 24 July, with the spell of fine weather hanging on, the Gala Sports Day was held. It had been preceded by an extensive advertising campaign which had stimulated a great interest in the racing events and the various sideshows. The course was laid out and the sideshows erected and by the time for the grand parade everything was ready. There were prizes for 'Best Dressed Lady', 'Best Bit of Boop', 'Most Humorous Male' and these attracted many entrants. Each country provided a sideshow of some description: New Zealand giving a Maori Haka; Canada, a cowboy and injun effort; Scotland, highland dancing; Australia, guess what? A two-up school!

There was a series of preliminary races in which each hut had entered two horses. The winner of each race qualified for the main event — the Klim Cup — which was ultimately won by Duff Gen followed by Airmen's Nightmare and Indiscretion. Horses moved on squares directed by the clerk of the course, who noted the results of each dice throw. A tote was run and we had bookies on the side while at the same time a bank was running for the conversion of cigarettes into paper money, a system adopted for convenience. The day, on the whole, was quite a success and credit was due to 'General' Booth and his assistants for organising such an extensive and enjoyable program.

The cricket season was well underway by this time. England beat New Zealand then Australia beat New Zealand. These two matches were followed by the second test, which England won easily. Late in August a combined dominions team defeated England and the season closed on 29 August when Australia suffered an overwhelming defeat at the hands of the Englishmen.

SHOT DOWN

On 4 August we started regular classes again for our Intermediate B.Sc. (Econ) from London University and we were fortunate to have three good teachers. We still had a lot of work to do, however, and settled down to some steady study. On 27 August we had another of the long searches which seemed to be a feature of this camp, and to while away the time we started up a large poker game while on parade. The Jerries' eyes bulged as they saw thousands of cigarettes changing hands. Two days later a big tunnel was discovered so once more we were up with the cock and onto the parade ground after a night of ceaseless counting. There was bags of flap (confusion) on the part of the Germans, with goons running here and there.

By 20 September cold frosty weather had set in and the rugby fans had the field almost to themselves. This was the period of fine cloudless mornings which seemed to us to herald the approach of a cold, early winter. We were wrong, however, for after about a month of this the rain set in — a steady monotonous drizzle, followed by incessant falls of wet snow which reduced the compound to a series of muddy paths and cold slushy pools.

On one of the days when I was feeling particularly depressed with POW life in general I put my feelings down on paper. I kept those thoughts and came across them among my papers after the war. What I wrote then was entitled somewhat sarcastically *Brave Thoughts on a Depressing Morning*. They went as follows:

It's cold — hell, it's cold. I roll over on my creaking boards and look towards the window. Through its frosted dimness I see once more — dull, hateful, my nemesis, the wire, close at hand, just through there, so close that you could almost touch it … .almost. You could almost jump over it from here, through the window and over it … almost.

Eight o'clock, sleep still clings, cloying brain cells … Years of this have dulled a man, slowing him up. Just an empty shell now. Eight o'clock. Must get up — why? God only knows. Why do anything in this place? Nothing matters. Months of it … oppressive barbed wire square. Life in an isolated kingdom, alienated from all that one holds dear — all that one loves. Cut off with the sharp finality of a knife through butter … Nothing matters.

Chapter 23

Feet on the cold floor, shambling uncertainly forward. Scratching mussy head, dulled with sleep ... Another day. Cold, wet, winter always worse. The fire is going — just. Everything is dirty. Why, oh why, must the day start like this?

This life hits hardest now ... In the early morning when everything is cold and dirty, and the wire leers at you and mocks you from the outside. Just through there, through that window. You could almost be out and over it before the guard had time to get his machine gun lined up ... almost. If you got caught there, hanging spreadeagled on the wire they'd tear you wide open ... Bullets hurt. Death is all right but to be wounded, scarred, mutilated!

The room smells; sweaty bodies, dirty clothes, stale smoke, mustiness. The cold lends a sharpness of outline to familiar objects. A dirty pan, fat congealed, like a grimy king sitting squat in a kingdom of greasy pots, large and small, all dirty. Clothes hanging up to dry strung forlornly along the roof. Clothes to dry; dirty pots; a deck of cards; rumpled blankets. Sixty men eat, drink, play, love, hate ... yes, live between these four walls in a space which would normally house a dozen or so cows during winter months.

I hate this place, now cold and empty, without even the warmth of human movement. Just through that window is the wire, eight feet high, then a tangled mess of virulent barbs and another eight foot fence. Ten running steps, six seconds to climb over, another six to make cover, then ... freedom — perhaps brief but still freedom.

But vacillation, vague indecision. Bullets bit deep. Who'd want to die hanging mutilated on a high barbed-wire fence? You could almost do it though ... almost!

About this time rumours began to circulate regarding repatriation but they were treated with the usual disdain accorded this type of gen by the kriegies. Within a week, however, things began to move and 14 of the boys including Bill left for Thorn, a medical camp in Poland not far away. Imagine our surprise then when, within a few days, the Germans announced that the first three boatloads of repatriated prisoners had arrived in England! That was the quickest work we had ever known any government to do. Two weeks!

On 5 October with our compound being now full, K Lager (a 'lager' was a compound used to contain prisoners) was opened and occupied by a batch of new kriegies. I began to keep a watch out for my pal Bob Blair who, I judged, would probably now be on ops. My wounds were all healed by now and I felt no ill effects from them, but I was keen to know what had become of the shrapnel that had been in my liver two years ago, so I applied for an X-ray. It showed that there was now only one piece near my liver and it seemed to have moved slightly higher and become lodged against the lower rib. The other one had just disappeared.

Late in October notice began to be taken of a spiritualist cum prophet cum magician (Nobby Clark) whose fame soon spread far and wide. It was soon obvious that here we had another Alfie James, wearing a different mantle perhaps and singing a different song, but working with the same psychological tools and achieving similar results. He preached 'war over on December 12' and of course he held his supporters until that date, after which he was spurned even by his former friends. It is remarkable how much influence a man like him can have on 2000 gullible aircrew.

By 7 November the lights were so bad and my eyes so sore that I stopped studying altogether and took up chess. At the same time all the boys from Barth who had left Sagan more than a year previously turned up again and were installed in K Lager, adjoining ours. Around this time the Germans approached the Canadians in the camp and told them that they were prepared to give preferential treatment in return for the similar treatment of prisoners of war in Canada. This offer, however, was declined by the senior Canadian, who decided that we should all stick together.

Dirty weather began to set in now and as 12 December was fast approaching and most of the prisoners were interested in Nobby Clark's date, the rumours began to fly thick and fast. In the first week of December there had been three or four meaty rumours each day and news began to roll in from independent sources confirming Nobby's date. Bets were made and speculation in the camp ran high. And all this was the work of one man. I think he must have read *The Road to Endor*. Well, 12 December sailed by and Nobby sailed out of the public eye. He was later repatriated as 'mentally unsound'.

Chapter 23

I suppose it is in the nature of man to be speculative and probably nowhere was this opportunity more aptly demonstrated than by reference to the amount of betting that went on in prison camp where news was scarce and not always reliable. Perhaps the fact that the wagers would, for the most part, be settled in the future after a return to civilisation, made it easier to undertake them. Additionally, one could see the inevitable optimism creeping into those bets that were undertaken; in most cases it was the pessimists who won. When I look back at many of the bets which I, myself, had recorded in my diary, and none of which were ever honoured after the war, I realise that we really did not have much of an idea of the situation. I won most of my bets by taking the pessimistic view. Most prisoners would have the war won and themselves repatriated within a year.

CHAPTER 24

THIRD CHRISTMAS IN PRISON, 1943

On 19 December 1943 the first show in the new theatre was presented. It was a comedy, *The Rotters*, and was followed quickly by the pantomime *Cinderella*. Both of these plays drew appreciative audiences and they provided a good commencement to the festive season. The next three days were given up to preparing Christmas decorations and planning Christmas feasts with whatever goodies had been saved for this special occasion. We had laid down a brew for Christmas Eve and it proved very successful and formed a prelude to our visits from hut to hut later in the night, singing and carrying on generally as much as the cold Baltic night allowed.

Christmas Day dawned fine and in marked contrast to most of its predecessors. The war news that was filtering through was getting better and better and the faces of the kriegies showed it. It was definitely looking as though the next year — now not so far away — could see an end to the conflict.

Jock Alexander, who considered himself one of the realists, said to me, 'Well, Alex, I think there's a chance that next Christmas may be our last in prison.'

'So you think the end might come in 1945?' I said.

'Maybe earlier,' he replied. 'Depends really on when the Allies decide to open their second front. The Yanks are thrusting into Italy and also giving the Jap navy a thrashing, the Allied forces are massing in Britain for the invasion, the Ruskis are now pushing strongly westwards, and the bombing must be starting to have a serious effect on German industrial production and on civilian morale. It seems as though it won't be long before the Russians are breathing down the

Germans' necks at Heydekrug and forcing an evacuation of our camp. What do you think?'

'Yes,' I mused. 'I suppose when you add it all up things are looking much brighter than this time last year. Let's hope you're right.'

The Americans were thrusting northwards from their foothold on Italy, the Allied forces in Britain were massing for the invasion to come and the Russians were advancing strongly from the east. In fact it was not long before the close proximity of the northern Russian Army would force the evacuation of our camp. Added to all these land-based successes was merciless and constant pounding by day and by night of the German mainland by massed fleets of Allied aircraft.

On New Year's Eve the snow lay deep on the ground and it was a fine, clear night. It was, incidentally, the first New Year's Eve on which I have ever sat an exam, and I hoped the last. I raced through the Economics paper and literally ran out of the examination room in order to get back to the boys before the brew ran out. It turned out to be too weak, however, so we went on the 'scrounge' and ended up getting quite merry on other brews. We finished a highly amusing and very enjoyable night by playing rugby in the snow.

From 10 to 15 January the weather was really cold and we got in about three or four days of good skating before a long thaw set in and reduced the compound to a slushy mess, in which state it remained for several weeks. It was during this period that Dave Fraser, in response to a request by POW air force officers, left for Barth as a batman to the officers there, hoping to find a chance to escape.

The first letter from my observer, Bill, arrived on 2 February and in it he told of his trip back through Sweden with the first repatriation group, his reception upon arrival in England, and his feelings and impressions on seeing once more his home which, a month previously, had seemed so far away. It made us envious, of course, though we were glad to learn that things had not changed so much in some respects and one could still enjoy oneself.

The air Battle of Berlin was raging intensely about this time and seemed to us to be building up to the Second Front. We were disappointed, of course, as we had been many times previously, that it had not yet taken place, and in spite of the optimistic statements of many of the new kriegies we were beginning to wonder if it would ever come. What gave the general situation a rosy appearance were the amazing successes of the Russian troops all along the line. It was a bad winter for Germany.

On 7 February, Ken Buchan from Subiaco arrived. Things started to happen rapidly and I soon had two sets of examinations on my hands — the Intermediate B.Sc. (Econ.) from London University and the English Matriculation examination. My matriculation record from Western Australia, which I had to present in order to qualify for the university, had not arrived in time so I sat the exam a second time. Curiously enough I took them in that order so legally I sat the London Inter before I had qualified for entrance. At this time, also, I enrolled in and completed my study for the special social studies examination set by Oxford University for Prisoners of War.

On 10 March, Dave and his party returned from Barth with some truly amazing stories. I found them hard to believe but evidence in the form of Dave's court martial sheet supported their tales.

Dave told me, 'As I was a flight sergeant I wasn't about to become a batman to any officer. I told them that I had volunteered to go to Barth because the chances of escaping seemed better than at Heydekrug. The stuffy, rank-conscious RAF senior officers took offence at what they considered my insubordination and they placed me on a court martial charge and sent me back to Heydekrug. I am now, at least for a while, an aircraftsman, having been reduced to the ranks by those silly bastards. They need reminding that it's every airman's duty to try to escape.' The charges were dropped after the war.

Soon after this came rumours of tents being erected in the compound. It seemed that the strength of the camp was eventually to be raised to 8000 and because the Germans were short of building materials the full accommodation could be made up only by the use of large marquees. Although this was only a rumour to begin with, it turned out ultimately to be true, the first big marquee being occupied on 10 May.

In March two new societies sprang up in the camp — La Société Francaise and Der Deutsch Verein, both of which proved popular and entertaining. I found them both useful in improving my French and German. We achieved our aim in La Société when, two months later, we produced our first French play — *L'Anarchiste Dupont* by E. G. Clark — which was received with enthusiastic applause.

On 9 April our combine of 10 persons, which had remained together almost two years (a record I think, for a combine as large as that), was at last split, or rather deprived of one member. Rocky got word of his commission and, with several other Canadians in the same boat, was sent to Stalag Luft III at Sagan. These commissions were granted after almost three years and came as a surprise for many of them. Possibly it was part of a scheme to pacify indignant kriegies who considered that to cut a prisoner off from all possible promotion and increases in pay was heavily penalising a man who was silly enough to join early and unlucky enough to be shot down early. My eventual lot was to be promoted to warrant officer. All my other ex-trainee friends were promoted to flight lieutenant while in Germany.

Two days later we had a small demonstration. Several pamphlets of obvious propaganda that the Germans had sent into the compound were publicly burned on the parade ground to show them that we were not inclined to lap it up. No more pamphlets came in. On the same day we got the news that Odessa had fallen, which won me a bottle of Haig whisky which I never received. At Christmas time I had bet that it would fall before 30 April 1944 so I really didn't have very much to spare and towards the end I was wondering whether Stalin could keep up his phenomenal progress. His advance across the southern sector was rapid, but was exceeded only a few months later when his big spring offensive opened up on a wide front in White Russia.

On 15 April more rumours began to float around concerning the repatriation of three-year prisoners. It was said that negotiations were almost complete and that something would soon come off. Several letters had been received from England containing the same information. Like almost everything else, though, it ultimately blew over and we gradually forgot it. After several false alarms fed, no doubt, by the unreasoning optimism of the long-time kriegies, we were beginning to feel rather pessimistic about schemes to repatriate prisoners and were focussing more on the ever increasing chances of the invasion coming from across the sea. News of the stepping up of the RAF bombing of the western French sea ports, particularly in the Pas de Calais area, was received with increasing interest.

CHAPTER 25
THE INVASION, 1944

On 19 April we were paraded at the usual time in the evening but we found that instead of the usual 10 guards or so, we had well over 40. There was a postern (guard) between each room and they all had their rifles at the ready and looked very jittery. There were also heavy machine guns on tripods mounted at several points around the compound and a few submachine guns carried by some of the guards. This had never happened before. We soon knew the cause of this.

The German lager fuhrer (compound leader) came on parade and brought with him an interpreter. He first read an order in German, which was then translated into English by the interpreter and again read, this time in English by the lager fuhrer to the assembled prisoners.

The captain announced his message in a loud voice. 'Leute!' (people) he said, 'the German High Command announces that yesterday in Camp Stalag Luft III at Sagan, 50 British prisoners were shot while attempting to escape.' His message was read out as a warning to other prisoners. As the details became known, it became obvious from the number of deaths that the prisoners were not shot while attempting to escape. It was also obvious that the Germans had increased the number of heavily armed guards because of the possibility of a mass demonstration by the prisoners and perhaps their action was justified. The shooting amounted to murder and later we learned that the order to shoot the escapees was given directly by Hitler.

Before the lager fuhrer could finish his announcement the prisoners started booing. The noise grew to a crescendo and continued for several minutes and the whole situation was looking very nasty indeed, with the German guards becoming very nervous and fingering their weapons. Eventually the German officer, unable to continue, threw his speech to the ground in a rage and stomped off the parade ground while Dixie Dean, our camp leader, moved to the centre and proceeded to try to calm the mob. It took a long time but eventually the parade dispersed and the German soldiers then did likewise.

Thus did we learn about what later became known as the Great Escape, which became enshrined in a novel of that name by an Australian, Paul Brickhill. A film of the same name was subsequently made. The loss of life, we discovered subsequently, was 50 prisoners who had all been murdered after recapture. Many of the German officers and men involved in the shooting were brought to justice at the Nuremberg crime trials and subsequently executed.

We celebrated Anzac Day with sports and a brew, the Aussies coming over from K Lager to take part. The day, which was a fine one, concluded with an Anzac concert in the theatre.

On 26 May came the presidential debate for the Literary and Debating Society, the motion being that 'This house prefers the past to the present'. I had been asked to stand for the committee with three others, and consequently we had to speak in the debate. Our positions on the committee were unopposed and so we were elected automatically, the only battle being between Dicky Beck and Nobby Hall, who were both standing for president. Dicky was elected by a large majority and we commenced what turned out to be the longest term of office of any committee of the society.

On 3 May I again spoke, this time as a supporter, in the first debate of our term of office. The motion was 'This house believes that the female of the species is deadlier than the male'. We were defending the honour of the absent female and we defeated the motion by a considerable majority. On 15 May an inter-compound debate that we had arranged with K Lager was held in that lager, our team soundly defeating the K Lager team. The motion was that 'This house considers that the woman's place is in the home'. Another debate we had arranged with the Americans of E Lager was postponed indefinitely after several abortive attempts to get the Yanks across to our lager.

We were now well into 1944 and still no invasion. May 14 was the date I had given for the invasion in the sweep we were running, so I said goodbye to my cigarettes and gave up trying to puzzle out the end of the war. That day, for the first time, our lager's softball team played the Yanks in their own lager and won the game 8–0. I was on third base but I had not a ball to field the whole day. Andy Cowan pitched an excellent game, holding the Yanks down to a one-hit shutout, and we left the American lager in good spirits.

On the night of 23 May the combined entertainments of our camp presented an all-star show entitled *For One Night Only*. It was produced specially for the YMCA representative who was paying us a visit. This year being the anniversary of the founding of the YMCA, it had been previously decided that we should stage a show of some kind to express our thanks for the way in which they had helped us since we had been prisoners. All entertainments on the camp were represented and the show was excellently compered, making the night a memorable one.

On 5 June Der Fuhrer declared Rome an open city and it was now plain that Kesselring's Army was retreating rapidly before the new Allied offensive. This was not the only front on which the German armies were withdrawing. Although things seemed quiet in Russia it was plain from the German front line bombing that the peace was due any day to be rudely shattered by the thunder of advancing Russian guns. Things on the French coast also seemed to be building up. The Allies had been bombing France intensively now, for many months, and the long awaited invasion seemed imminent. The Pas de Calais area seemed to be a focal point.

The next day it came — the event upon which we had been building our hopes now for years and which at times had seemed so near, at others so far, was now taking place. We had bled all new prisoners for news of the preparations in England. Our strategists (that includes almost everyone in camp) had often given the date and place for the mission; our super-strategists (only a few this time) had even suggested that it was all part of the war of nerves — that there would not be an invasion. All talk of the war had centred on the invasion for it meant a big step on the road home for us.

Well, it was here — the momentous 6 June! The news came through from the kitchen that it had just been announced over the German radio. At first we would not believe it, thinking it to be just another of the many rumours, but after an hour or so confirmation came from the German guards so we accepted it. When the truth of it became apparent the fellows threw their hats in the air and cheered hysterically. I couldn't bring myself even to cheer. I had been expecting it for so long that I merely accepted it and turned back to my book. I couldn't help feeling that that is the way I would accept the news of the Armistice. Displaying passion or sentiment in a crowd is a thing I just can't easily do.

Then there were doubts. New prisoners told us that Churchill had said that there would be many feints. Perhaps this was merely the first. Time would tell. But then it soon became obvious that it was the first great Allied landing from which many mechanised armies were eventually to sweep across France towards the German border. And so the biggest event of our prison life had taken place.

The first week was a trying one but it soon became evident that Jerry could not knock us off the mainland. He admitted himself that our troops had a firm hold but maintained that the German aim was to force a major battle upon us in the early stages. When he had decisively beaten us and knocked our armies off the Normandy beach-head, he would transfer his troops to Poland where the Russian threat to East Prussia and Germany proper was becoming very serious. Having defeated the Russians he would then bomb Britain into submission with his new secret weapon the V.1. (flying bomb), which he had produced a few days after the invasion. Just how ignominiously he had failed in every phase of this plan became evident two months later when the American and English armies swept on past Paris, headed eastward, and the great Russian steamroller once again got underway, headed westward.

On the night of 12 June I was awakened about midnight by a good deal of movement in the hut and I dressed and went to the window, which was lit up by a red glare. A loud crackling greeted my ears and great tongues of flame were springing from the theatre.

The German guard captain for the night soon realised that his guards could not hope to quell the flames without the aid of the kriegies and other German soldiers.

'All prisoners!' he shouted, 'Raus. Komme. Hilfe.'

The prisoners flooded out of their barracks, anxious to prevent the fire from devouring their precious theatre.

'Get a bucket and form a chain,' shouted Jock over the noise of the flames and the Germans and the kriegies. 'We want one here,' he said pointing to the entrance, 'and one here on the northern corner.'

Blackie called out from the southern side. 'There are flames coming from the back entrance. We want another chain here before it gets away from us!'

The bucket chains were rapidly formed from the wash-house to the theatre and in no time things were brought under control by the guard captain, who thanked the kriegies. The ironic twist to the incident was that just as the flames were brought under control the first few drops appeared from the large fire hose manned by the camp fire squad. The night itself was memorable not so much because of the fire as because we were allowed to roam around the camp unhindered in the dark for the first time in our prison life.

I have read a book dealing with the future of education by Sir Richard Livingstone and I came across what seemed to me a rather too indulgent statement which ran something like this: 'It is easy for men to trust each other when they have lived and worked together for months under one roof; the suspicion based on ignorance melts away.' A little reflection on this leads me to doubt the truth of this assertion. Perhaps — if qualified by the phrase 'under normal conditions' — it would have a truer ring. I am convinced that when men are herded together in squalid surroundings, divorced from the conventions and superficial embellishments of normal social life, human nature drops the thin veneer of civilisation and assumes once more the true animal instincts which thousands of years of communal life have failed to erase. This is not to say, of course, that under normal conditions these baser instincts are not capable of being suppressed. Let us give them the benefit of the doubt and say, rather, that in most human beings there is an inherent desire for the advantages and corresponding duties and obligations of the communal life rather than a mere capacity for it.

About this time we held a two-day boxing tournament in the centre of the Yank compound. There were some very good bouts, but the event which attracted most attention was the much advertised kriegie welterweight championship bout between John Tracey (RAF), the present title holder, and 'The Bearded Marvel' (USAF), the hush-hush American challenger. There was a great deal of betting on the fight and most of the RAF men were confident that Tracey's particularly vicious right would send the Yank down for the count, while most of the Americans were equally confident that their Pittsburgh boy would hand out a surprise to his opponent. At the end of the first round Tracey brought his right into play for the first time and sent the Yank down to his knees, just on the gong. Tracey's round, definitely. Second round, honours even. In the third round, however, the Yank came good and closing in began to gain point after point. His in-fighting definitely won him the bout for he pounded Tracey's ribs until he was hardly able to defend himself. When the result was announced the Americans went mad with joy and the RAF compound looked rather glum. That fight was the subject of discussion for many months afterwards whenever fight fans got together.

A week or so after this I booked an interview with the padre and on being admitted to his room one morning began to explain my problem. I was dissatisfied with orthodox Christianity as a religion and after putting it on trial for a year or so had decided, before I finally went cold on it, to give the official representative of the Church a chance to defend his faith. Much to my surprise I found his views on life very similar to mine except for one very important stumbling block. He regarded man as endowed with the capacity for divine grace, as an incarnate morsel of the Godhead. I regarded man as the most recent term in an ever-growing geometrical series. The padre's attempt to defend the Christian tenets was not very spirited. Perhaps, after all, he realised the fundamental truth underlying Aldous Huxley's assertion that Christianity is essentially a religion to satisfy visceratonics and that the religion for the cerebretonic is mysticism. At any rate, I left with the padre's recommendation to follow whatever creed appealed to me, so long as I was satisfied within myself that I had given it due thought.

On 21 June 1944, Stalin started again with a big offensive and got going pretty well — so well, in fact, that by 15 July he was threatening the vicinity of our camp and soon rumours began to circulate to the effect that we should soon be evacuated. Rumour soon became fact and we were told definitely that we should be leaving on Saturday. Thus began the pre-evacuation panic.

CHAPTER 26
STALAG 357 THORN: POLAND, 1944

With the Russians advancing rapidly towards us we had been anticipating a move for about a week and now our fears had materialised. We were given instructions to prepare to leave at a moment's notice.

The hauptmann came into our hut and announced, 'We are ordered to be ready to move at a moment's notice because the military situation is very uncertain. So I'm giving you warning to have all your things packed and ready to go immediately the order comes through.' He was probably not aware (and neither were we for that matter) that we were being sent to north-western Germany, along with all the other prisoners in German hands, to be used as hostages if needs be.

There followed a frantic packing of kit and selection of 'necessary' articles, as we were to take only what we could carry. The Australian 'bluey bag' made from a blanket gained rapid popularity and when we finally left Heydekrug the majority of the prisoners carried their kit this way.

Combines who had accumulated reserve stocks of food during the winter months were compelled to leave the greater part of it behind and all food and other articles which could not be taken were thrown into the two big latrines in order to ensure that if we could not have them at least the Germans would not be able to enjoy them.

The German administration of the camp seemed to be in complete chaos. The office was sadly disorganised, hundreds of pounds worth of technical books and classical records lay on the floor of the library and gramophones and musical instruments lay discarded on the tables. The cigarette values of small portable articles such as watches and rings skyrocketed overnight because cigarettes were difficult to carry in large numbers. Medical supplies from the sick bay were issued to separate parties in case of casualties from strafing or bombing by aircraft while in transit. There were 38,000 Red Cross food parcels in the vorlager and the commandant did not provide transport either for these or for communal camp property such as sports or educational equipment or Red Cross clothing. So there was a lot of valuable (to a kriegie) stores and equipment left to the wolves (human)!

It was sad to see all the equipment which often made the difference between boredom and useful activity of great value to them in many ways just jettisoned. It not only deprived the kriegies of really good and useful equipment but it had a psychological effect when they thought of what they would not be able to engage in in the immediate future. Apart from the frustration of seeing their favourite sports or other activities suddenly swept from under them they were also confused as to where they were going to next.

We were certain that the Heydekrug evacuation was due to the rapid advance of the Russian troops, which were only a matter of 20 miles away. Soldiers and civilians alike were rushing to find transport to flee the Russians. They had little doubt as to what would happen to them were they caught. It was a no-win situation for everybody.

The first party to leave the camp were the Yanks, who were bound for Stalag Luft 1V at Stettin. They pulled out on Friday night after having exchanged almost all their food for our cigarettes. Taken collectively, the Yanks were a peculiar group and in this instance they were giving away food in order to be able to carry more cigarettes. We, who gave our stomachs and health first priority, were only too glad to accommodate them. We heard later that the Yanks had embarked at Memel and arrived at Stettin after an extremely uncomfortable journey in the hold of a cargo boat, and a subsequent forced march from the docks to their camp.

We fared somewhat better. Five o'clock Saturday afternoon found us standing by in the main compound and within an hour we were marching to the station, packs on our backs containing as much food as we could carry and the bare minimum of clothing. We had called at the Red Cross store on our way through the vorlager and gathered as much solid food as we thought it possible to take without breaking down. When we arrived at the Heydekrug railway station we found it packed with refugees — old men, rickety-looking children and tired-looking women who were awaiting relief trains and who were certainly not pleased to see the prisoners being evacuated before themselves. We were herded into cattle trucks (40 hommes, 8 chevaux) which were partitioned off into barbed wire cages each holding 20 men. Our boots were removed by the Germans and at 11.30 pm on Saturday we pulled out, bootless and cold, headed south.

We passed through Tilsit, Insterberg and Allenstein, which were fated to fall into Russian hands soon after the Russian generals commenced their great winter offensive of January 1945. They rapidly carved off great slices of Brandenberg and Pomerania as well as Silesia and East Prussia. On the way south we were halted for an hour or so beside a goods train on which appeared to be living a family of Russians from Leningrad. We passed them some food and I managed to get across a few of the Russian phrases that I had learned in case we were overrun by the Russians. The women handed us a peace offering of a piece of smelly meat and thenceforth we lapsed into Deutsch in which we seemed to get on much better.

We finally arrived at Thorn, the great Polish fortress, after an eventful train journey of approximately 24 hours. From Thorn station we were marched through the town and out to a prison camp some two miles beyond. By this time it was dark and we were directed immediately to a reception barrack where we soon fell asleep, exhausted and tired. Early the next morning we were searched along with 3000 army personnel who had joined us from stalags further to the south. A good percentage of the soldiers were Aussies, many of them from the 2/11th and 2/28th WA battalions including a few whom I had known back in Perth.

So now we were installed once more many miles from the Russian columns with the prospect of liberation once more far away. In point of fact, despite Stalin's proximity to Heydekrug he did not take it until November, four months after we had been evacuated. Still, the next thing we could look forward to was an advance on Thorn, towards which the Russian armies seemed to be pushing.

SHOT DOWN

It seemed to us at the time that the Germans had conducted the evacuation of Heydekrug quite efficiently considering the suddenness of the move but much later, looking back, we came to the conclusion that they had panicked us unduly, probably in the hopes that it would have the effect that it actually did. Apart from the things we dumped in the latrines, there certainly was a lot of food and clothing left at Heydekrug which fell into the hands of the German Army and the civilians. A complaint was subsequently lodged with Geneva and we were informed later that the German commandant was to be punished for failing to provide transport. It didn't do us any good at the time, however.

It was at Thorn (Stalag 357) that we were introduced to swap shops and blowers, two creations which contributed to the partial alleviation of the vicissitudes of kriegie life.

Swap shops, as their name implies, are stalls or shops where it is possible to swap one article for another, from pipe-cleaners to Red Cross food. The generally accepted medium of exchange was cigarettes and a levy of one cigarette was charged by the swap shop proprietor for each swap. They became very popular and proliferated throughout the camp.

Blowers struck us immediately as being extremely useful devices for 'brewing up,' for they generated a remarkable amount of heat with very little fuel. Made from large empty Red Cross milk (Klim) tins with a hand-wound rotary fan attached, they could heat a litre of water to boiling point using a sheet of newspaper as fuel. Because his brew is one of the nearest things to a kriegie's heart we all made it our aim for our combine to acquire a blower as soon as possible.

A source of constant amusement for the army boys was the strange species of slang peculiar to the RAF. We had become dependent upon a few small words to express our thoughts. One-syllable words like 'gash', 'gen', 'duff' encouraged a dangerous mental laziness, and a kriegie, instead of selecting the *mot juste,* explained himself with an RAF slang word.

For example, I came across Herbie explaining to one of the army boys from his home town, Adelaide, who was taken in Crete, what happened to a new pilot on the squadron: 'He was a sprog from Melbourne and first day on ops he flew as tail-end Charlie, took some flak and pranged his kite and bought it.'

'What the hell are you talking about?' said his friend.

'I'm telling you, he was killed,' replied Herb.

The army laughed at our jargon; I was inclined to regard its increasing popularity with apprehension. I imagined that we kriegies, who for perhaps four or five years had not been forced to temper our language at all, were going to commit many faux pas before we finally settled down once more into the order of civilian life. All I hoped was that those who happened to overhear any chance epithets that I may drop would be tolerant enough to excuse me on the grounds of 'extenuating circumstances'.

It was at Thorn that we first saw the strange vapour trails in the clear blue summer sky which subsequently became so familiar to all and sundry after the war. We did not know at the time, but in retrospect it was obvious, that we were witnessing the vapour trails of the first military jet aircraft in the world. The Germans were almost ready to put their first jet-powered Messerschmitts into service. They were using the relatively quiet Polish skies for their tests. In the event, they elected to use the aircraft before they were fully operational and because of that lost most of them in the early days of their operation. This was towards the end of the war. Had the German industrial machine been capable of producing this aircraft in quantity well before 1945 things would have been much harder for the Allies.

On the noteworthy 20 July came the event which, to our mind, had it been successful, might well have meant the end of the war. A German colonel attempted unsuccessfully to take the Fuhrer's life. Of course the camp was alive with rumours from then onward during the general administration clean-up, but the Fuhrer rapidly executed the ringleaders and many more, including the former hero General Rommel, who was given a pill to end it all.

But the news from the front itself was sufficient to keep us in good spirits with the Russians advancing rapidly in the east. The brief period we spent at Thorn (little more than three weeks of fine weather) provided a very pleasant interlude during which we swapped news and experiences with the army boys and even received a few visits from the Red Air Force. But alas, it came to an early end for we were soon evacuated en masse to central Germany. This time, however, the evacuation was conducted in a more organised fashion, with time to spare.

The ninth of August proved to be a fine summer's day, for which we were duly thankful because we were faced with an almost three-mile march to the Thorn railway station. We were entrained by midday and late in the afternoon we pulled out headed for our new camp, Fallingbostel, which was situated in the centre of a triangle, having as its three apexes Hannover, Hamburg and Bremen.

CHAPTER 27
FOURTH CHRISTMAS IN PRISON: FALLINGBOSTEL, GERMANY, 1944

We were heading for our last prison camp though we did not know it at the time. Over several months it gradually became clear that the Germans were pulling their prisoners back from the approaching Allied troops both in the east from the Russians, in the south from the Americans, and in the west from the British and Americans. They were moving them gradually to northern central Germany. Since they absorbed security forces and were a liability when it came to food and accommodation we concluded that they were regarded as important for some reason not quite clear.

But as the months passed it became crystal clear that the war for the Germans was lost and it was only Hitler's obstinacy preventing a settlement. Most of Hitler's generals would have preferred a negotiated ceasefire at this stage and they were in no doubt as to the severity of the surrender terms. Meanwhile the prisoners spent their time wondering what would be their ultimate fate.

'I'd like to know what they're going to do with us,' mused Jock. 'There's so many rumours going around these days. We're going to be used as human shields in a final showdown with the Wermacht (German Army). Now I can't see that happening even with that madman still in charge. There may be plans for us all to be shot as a last resort. If he did that in cold blood with the escapees at Sagan I s'pose he could do it with us.'

Suggy broke in with, 'The strongest rumour is that he'll move us all into one big group and use us as hostages in surrender negotiations.'

'But,' I interjected, 'there's one other possibility and that is that the German High Command may somehow get rid of Hitler and negotiate a surrender as soon as possible. Who knows when that may happen?'

Christmas 1944 was approaching and the food situation was still a matter of concern. Some of us had saved enough from our spasmodic and hybrid issues over the previous three months to ensure us a meal which would at least be better than we could have expected on German rations alone, but no-one had very much food and the prospects of a cheery Christmas were really not too bright. Even the military news was not so cheery for the Allied advances had slowed down in the inclement weather and our hopes for a Christmas at home had long been dashed.

We were saved by the gong, you might say, as on Boxing Day some Red Cross food arrived from Sweden which tided us over for a while. All in all, including a brief spell of fine, clear, cold weather, our Christmas was not as bad as it had threatened to be. Because our food store was the result of enforced hardship and saving in the past, it was enjoyed just that much more. Because all of our entertainment had to be provided without the artificial stimulus usually given by a raisin brew, it was more solid and real and, therefore, more enjoyable.

Meanwhile we were eagerly watching the progress of von Runstedt's troops, who had broken out westward in the Ardennes. The Germans in their papers claimed this as the big German winter offensive which would turn the tide of the war. We welcomed it because we thought that if von Rundstedt brought his forces out into the open it would give our armies the chance of smashing him and thereby possibly shortening the course of the war. Because of this we were glad to welcome any good weather which must give our tactical air force the chance they wanted to hit the enemy.

Nevertheless von Runstedt had immediate success. He pushed well into the Allied lines while the foul weather denied Allied air forces any opportunity of supporting their ground troops and harassing the enemy. The Allied airborne troops were overrun and had to fall back with severe casualties. Then the weather began to improve and the Allied forces gained the ascendancy. By the end of February, von Runsted was back to where he had started and his great drive had come to nought. He had, however, given the Allies a severe mauling and had taken many prisoners to swell the millions of prisoners the Reich now held. Hitler was well aware that the treatment of these prisoners could be used as a threat and a possible bargaining tool in future negotiations for a surrender.

By this time many thousands of kriegies of all nations, from southern and western Germany, were marching northwards and eastwards clogging up the roads and adding significantly to the general confusion. The exodus from Fallingbostel to join the other marching prisoners commenced in March 1945 and consisted of several columns comprising approximately 12,000 men. Some years after the end of hostilities a comprehensive and well-researched book, *The Last Escape*, describing the Long March, as it became known, was written by John Nichol and Tony Rennell and published by Viking in 2002. It took more than half a century for the true story to emerge of the horrendous treatment of their prisoners by the Germans in the last six months of the war. But first, back to the camp.

It was still cold. The winter had not yet yielded its dominance. The frosts still heralded each day. But wood, previously always at a premium, was at last no longer in short supply. In fact it was even becoming plentiful as more and more prisoners left the camp. The result was that in some huts fires were burning continuously and heartily, a phenomenon unknown in the last three years. No longer was it necessary for me as *arbeitsfuhrer* to organise the wood-gathering work parties. Now it was simply a matter of gathering bed boards from an empty hut or of ripping off its side planking, or of pulling fence posts out of the ground and stripping the barbed wire from them. It seemed there was little point in conserving fuel since the ability to use it would soon be denied us.

So Fallingbostel, Stammlager 357, was being evacuated at last. Hut by hut and over an extended period of time, the large kriegsgefangenenlager was disgorging its human complement. With greatcoats (French, German or British, or whatever they could muster to keep their bodies warm) wrapped around them and an odd assortment of bags, packs, humpies and parcels in either or both arms, off they marched — or straggled, rather. From Fallingbostel alone 12,000 prisoners, split into columns of approximately 1000, spilled out onto the German countryside over a period of weeks. Many of the prisoners in camps in southern Germany had to march in the snow and some of them made small sleds on which they could pile their meagre belongings. The trouble was that the sled had to be pulled and when the snow ran out this became difficult.

Whither they were headed they did not know, though rumours were rife, of course. It is probable that even the Germans did not know, nor, it appeared, did they care very much. In fact the German guards, or many of them, appeared to have lost all interest in playing the role of captor and now and again one of them would disappear. He was presumed to have deserted and to be heading for home and family. Administration had broken down to the point where in some groups German officers were losing control of some of their troops and were shooting them for disobeying orders.

The Russians were advancing rapidly westwards, Patton's tanks were coming from the south at great speed to get to Berlin before the Russians, and in the west Montgomery's armoured divisions, having recovered from the winter setback at Arnhem, were slicing into the German armies that were now trying desperately but ineffectually to defend the Fatherland.

The main concern of the marching prisoners, apart from scrounging food from the devastated and war-torn countryside as they made their way slowly through it, was who would get to them first, the Russians or the Allies. The prospect of being 'liberated' by the Russians was not as appealing as one might think. Rumours were rife, as might be expected.

There was a rumour (later confirmed as correct) that the Germans were intending to march their prisoners to one great central assembly point where they would hold them as hostages while bargaining on the terms of surrender. It was revealed after the war that Hitler had ordered SS Generalleutnant Berger, Chief of Prisoner of War Affairs, to organise hundreds of thousands of Allied prisoners to undertake forced marches in severe weather towards a central point. There Hitler would use them as a bargaining weapon for negotiating the surrender terms. His alternative, if negotiations failed, was to shoot all the prisoners.

At his trial, at Nuremberg after the war, Berger testified that he slowed down the whole procedure in direct contravention of Hitler's orders so as to avoid having to give the order to shoot a quarter of a million prisoners. He was assisted by Eva Braun. He was no doubt thinking of the approaching day of reckoning. He was eventually acquitted in the post-war trials.

What I, and my fellow prisoners, did not know at the time was that the Allied High Command had considered this possibility and had resolved not to give way to Hitler but to insist on unconditional surrender, irrespective of what might happen to the prisoners. This would not have been good news for the prisoners, had they known, and would have caused great reaction from the British and American public had they known. In blissful ignorance, not knowing of the Allies' intentions, but harbouring serious thoughts about the situation, I decided to take matters into my own hands and make sure that I would end up on the right side of the Rhine by escaping and travelling west by myself.

THE LONG MARCH: GERMANY, 1945

It is officially estimated that in the middle of 1944 Germany held nine million prisoners. That number does not take into account the millions of Russian and Jewish prisoners that had been killed and murdered.

The prisoners on the Long March came from all quarters of the European continent in many different columns. Some of them had been on the march much longer than the Fallingbostel prisoners. The marches were long and arduous. The pressure on the prisoners to keep pushing on was unrelenting. Some POWs marched for more than 500 miles and were on the road for many months in severe cold. Many perished during the march. Those who could go on no longer and fell by the roadside were either shot by the guards or left to die. Others were shot by friendly fire as RAF planes attacked marching columns and villages. It is estimated conservatively that between 1500 and 2500 prisoners were killed on the march. The YMCA estimated that between September 1944 and May 1945 some 8348 British and American prisoners died in captivity.

We slept sometimes in barns and other makeshift civilian accommodation commandeered by the German guards and many a German farmer must have cursed the scavenging kriegies upon finding, after they moved off in the morning, that his chickens and vegetables were missing. At other times we slept in the open, always conscious of the strafing and bombing and the frenetic air activity. Every day bombs rained down on the countryside seemingly indiscriminately.

The emotions of the kriegies at this point were mixed. On the one hand they would mostly have preferred to find a nice hideout safe from the bombing and remain there until the hostilities were over — but how long would that take? On the other hand they were aware that every step took them closer to a reunion with all their mates and hopefully closer to the Allied armies. The latter prevailed and they trudged on.

It was not long before we were discarding equipment and clothing that became surplus to our basic needs because as the days went on our packs seemed to become heavier and heavier as we grew weaker and weaker. Under these circumstances our priorities were constantly changing.

Compared to the six months of planning and sweat that had gone into the Kirchain tunnel, these confused and insecure conditions made any escape seem so easy. On the other hand, stories were circulating (later confirmed as true) about escaping prisoners being shot or hanged from nearby trees when caught on the run by fanatical and desperate SS troops. So it would pay to be very careful. There was no doubt that general conditions were much more chaotic and life-threatening than in 1942. I wondered which alternative carried the least risk to life or limb — run or stay. I decided to run — most prisoners decided to stay.

My first escape from the marching column was short-lived. We had eaten horse that day. For some reason that eludes me, a horse was killed and we all had a piece of meat for the first time in a few days. I felt that with that fortification in my belly now was the time to act. *Carpe diem*! It was not difficult at all and I made my move by slipping into some dense bushes at the side of the road just about dusk. I went to ground as soon as I was a safe distance from the column. With my swag, I spent a reasonably comfortable night in some bushes and got on my way westward as soon as I could see where I was going.

Progress was fairly slow in daylight and concealment difficult, and on the second day I was recaptured by a small platoon of German regulars. They were retreating eastwards and were not in a very friendly mood when they challenged me. In fact I was rather concerned at first for my safety. They were a different class of soldier from the elderly prison guards we were used to and I decided that to attempt to escape again while in their custody would be foolhardy in the extreme for they would not hesitate to shoot.

The platoon commander asked me, 'Wer bist du?' (Who are you?) 'Wo kommst du her?' (Where did you come from?) I told him that I had escaped from a column of prisoners nearby. What saved me from deep trouble was the fact that many German soldiers had already given up their desire to fight and their sergeant was one of them. He told me that I was stupid and could easily have been shot.

'Gehen sie zuruck zu Ihrer spalte,' commanded the sergeant and I willingly complied as the column was nearby.

Thinking it over subsequently I realized that it was really stupid of me to go off into the woods on my own without a definite plan of escape. So I told the platoon commander that I had escaped from the Fallingbostel column which was nearby. In due course he returned me to the column, where I found myself in another group from Fallingbostel which had left a day or two after the group I was originally attached to

Herb Crump was in the column I had just joined and together we planned to escape when an opportunity presented itself.

We got chatting about how we could get out of our present situation as we were both uncomfortable marching into what was virtually the unknown. It was easy enough to escape because the march conditions were becoming more and more chaotic, but there were many facets of such a venture that needed careful consideration.

'I don't want to stay in this column,' said Herb. 'It feels like bad luck to me and I definitely don't want the Ruskis to catch us up. I don't trust the bastards.'

'I agree,' I said. 'But it's not going to be easy to get over to the other side. On foot, as we are, we'll eventually have to go through the German frontline where there might be some very angry German soldiers and then we'll have to go through the Allied front line where there may be some trigger-happy Limeys. Altogether it's not a pleasant prospect.'

Conditions were deteriorating rapidly and some of our guards deserted. The column continued with a reduced German staff for the most part to retain some kind of coherence. With communications now completely confused and almost non-existent the German commandant was pretty much on his own having been reduced to using pushbikes and his own car for his orders.

Next day we had an experience which heightened our resolve to leave the column and get heading west quickly. We had reached Gresse, just south of Lubeck, where we were given two Red Cross parcels each. It was a job to carry these because we were already weak and cluttered up with gear so we proceeded to eat as much as we could while marching.

Soon we were on our way again heavily laden with our newly acquired food. The sky was alive with aircraft of all kinds bombing and strafing. About midday nine rocket-equipped Typhoons appeared on the horizon. They flew past us very low on the port side and then they wheeled slowly around and swung back towards us. I felt my pulse start racing as I realised what was going to happen. Thinking that we were a column of German troops, they came in low to strafe. Their rockets were powerful and deadly.

I yelled out to Herbie, 'They're going to hit us!', and without further ado dived into a ditch beside the road. In an instant after the kriegies looked back at the Typhoons I had several bodies soon on top of me. My survival instincts, which had been sharply honed over the years, had not failed me and I had been the first to hit the dirt in the ditch. Many of the marching prisoners had not noticed that the Typhoons had swung around towards us and had been oblivious of the approaching danger. The rockets hit the road and exploded in the midst of and along the length of the column of prisoners, cutting a deadly swathe through the prisoners and guards in a crescendo of instant death, spraying blood and body parts everywhere.

The terrible noise of the rockets and cannon shells striking the road in a horrific few minutes merged with the roar of the aircraft engines and the screams and cries of the maimed and wounded. The carnage that those Typhoons inflicted in a few short minutes was unbelievable. Bodies were flung into the air. There were dead and dying prisoners and German guards strewn across the road in bloody confusion. One torso was found in a tree, minus limbs. A friend, who had been my combine partner in Stalag IIIE and used to sing to us so beautifully after lights out, was propped up against a tree minus both legs. He died soon after. Sixty Allied prisoners were killed and nearly one hundred seriously wounded. The casualties included Canadians, Australians, New Zealanders, South

Africans, Englishmen, Irishmen, Welshmen, Scots and one American. Some bodies and parts of bodies could not be identified.

Survivors were rushed to Gresse hospital. The bodies and pieces of the dead were later interned, after identification, in a communal grave dug in the local churchyard. Some of the victims had been prisoners more than four years and were so close to liberation.

After that, Herb and I decided that it was now or never and the following day we slipped away from the column, preferring to risk our necks on the run rather than take the risk of being strafed again. We realised how lucky we had been. We moved cautiously at first, avoiding civilians and soldiers alike, stealing food where we could, crossing fields and streams, keeping away from well-used thoroughfares, bedding down in bombed-out barns and generally keeping a very low profile. We had with us a large piece of white calico which was for waving at the appropriate time. It was eventually used to good effect at the right time!

For several days we moved westward, sometimes showing ourselves and scrounging food when we could not find any to steal. This we did increasingly as it became obvious that the whole situation had deteriorated and most German soldiers did not seem to care any more about fighting. Many of them had discarded their arms. We found that the ordinary German soldiers were not interested in us, particularly as we got closer to the front. We were, however, careful to check their uniforms before showing ourselves. We did not want to run foul of the Waffen SS so close to liberation.

On one occasion in a narrow laneway we had to step aside carefully to allow past a heavy dray drawn by two draught horses and crammed with German soldiers heading eastwards, away from the fighting. It seemed that they had given up any pretence of being soldiers anymore and were heading for home as fast as they could go. As they passed us they called out greetings and threw out bread loaves and hard biscuits, for which we were grateful.

On another occasion we came across a column of tiger tanks heading east. I spoke, maybe rather foolhardily in retrospect, to the German tank commander, who had stopped to take his bearings and had opened his turret for some fresh air.

I edged closer to the leading tank as the tank commander raised his turret. 'Who are you?' he asked as he wiped the sweat from his brow. It was already warming up.

'Good morning, Captain,' I answered. 'We are escaped British prisoners heading for no man's land and freedom. Do we have far to go to reach the front line?'

He hesitated for a minute then said, 'The British tanks are about 50 kilometres westwards and coming fast.' He was obviously not inclined to be friendly and I decided that I should terminate the conversation and move away from his space quickly.

'You bloody stupid fool,' said Herb when we were out of earshot. 'You could have got us shot. I can't believe you just did that. If I'd known you were going to talk to that bastard I would have stopped you.'

In retrospect I was inclined to agree with Herb. 'Yeah, sorry,' I replied. But now we knew how close the Allies were and we could make the necessary plans.

It was not long after that we could hear the sounds of sporadic gunfire, some of it obviously cannon as well as small arms, but there was really not the atmosphere of a fierce battle or a battle of any kind raging in this neck of the woods. Relative quiet seemed to have descended on the area and we became convinced that we were now in an extended no man's land, as all the German troops seemed to have disappeared and British troops were nowhere to be seen. German foot soldiers and armoured columns were retreating rapidly. There seemed to be a distance of several miles between the two front lines. The only disturbance was from the innumerable aircraft — Typhoons, Spitfires, Hurricanes, Mustangs, Mosquitos and others which screamed overhead and criss-crossed one another in their search for moving targets.

At this point we came to a small stone bridge across a small creek. We could hear what appeared to be sounds of tanks approaching so we decided that it was time for us to exercise caution and went to ground or rather to water at the site of the bridge.

'Have you got that white flag?' I asked Herb. 'The important thing is when we show it. We can't show our position too soon in case it's a

German detachment, but we can't delay too long in case there are some trigger-happy Brits in the leading tanks.'

'Trouble is,' said Herb, 'that I don't really know the difference between the tiger tanks of the Germans and the British tanks. We're going to have to take a bit of a punt. We'd better be right.'

We slid down the embankment and took cover under the bridge to await events. We were not too keen at that point on revealing ourselves or walking over the bridge where we would have had no cover if fired upon. We felt that it was imperative to establish that we were among friends before we waved our white flag. We heard the rumble of a tank approaching and held our breath. Was it British or German?

CHAPTER 29
FREEDOM, 1945

We did not have long to wait before a tank rumbled round the street corner about half a mile beyond our bridge. Herb had readied our white sheet and after satisfying ourselves that the tank was friendly we gingerly held our breath and emerged from our hiding place, brandishing our white flag and praying that the tank crew were not trigger-happy.

Those first few moments of apprehensive exposure passed and we stood there as the tank lumbered up, now followed by a column of other tanks, and stopped. The turret opened and out popped the tank commander.

'Who are you chaps?' he asked.

'We're Aussies,' I replied. 'We escaped a couple of weeks ago and we were making our way towards the front line. I guess we've made it.'

'You sure have,' he said with a grin. 'But before we go any further convince me that you are who you say you are. We have to be careful.'

A short quiz session was enough to prove our bona fides, and then he asked us, 'Have you seen any German troops recently?'

We described in detail the German tank detachment of the day before, but I assumed that our information would already be outdated. Then he reached down into the belly of the tank and produced a half-empty bottle of cognac, a packet of cigarettes and two large bars of chocolate. 'Get on the outside of that lot,' he said. 'You look half-starved, which you probably are.'

A friendly wave, down with the turret and the tank rumbled on, leading its now long retinue of tanks like a mother duck. Still in a daze Herb and I hugged each other, danced around like madmen and finally sank down by the side of the road as it began to dawn on us that we were at last free men.

It took some time for it to sink in that for us the war was at last over and we were safe.

'It's all over Herb,' I said. 'But I really can't believe it.'

'Same here,' said Herb. 'Won't Kit get a surprise when I call her from London.'

'I'll call my mum as soon as I can,' I told him. 'She'll get a big surprise — she'll have no idea of where I am or what has happened to me.'

'Well,' said Herb, 'we'd better obey the tank commander and get on the outside of these goodies.'

We were in no hurry. It took us about an hour to finish the cognac and chocolate, cheering and waving to the passing troops as we adjusted our minds to our new status. So much activity was going on in front and around us as the ground troops appeared, accompanying the tanks, that we were not yet really able to appreciate the difference between being imprisoned and being free. It was dawning on us slowly.

About midday we rose and walked somewhat unsteadily up the road to the corner where we had first sighted the tank. By this time the village was alive with British troops. We walked into a large German home on the corner to confront a rather frightened farmer who had a wife and two daughters. To their obvious relief our requests were relatively simple and capable of being met. We wanted a hot bath, some clean clothes, a good meal and a sleep on a comfortable bed between white sheets — in that order. The farmer and his wife rushed around and lost no time in complying. By mid-afternoon, clean and replete and assisted by the soporific effect of the cognac, we fell into a deep sleep which lasted until the following morning.

By early morning we had made our plans get a lift back to the front if possible (it was by now several miles further east), commandeer a car from a freshly overrun village (those occupied for some time would already be bereft of cars), scrounge some petrol from the troops and drive back to Paris where we would sell the car, have a good time and paint the town red with some of the proceeds, then back to England still with some money left in our pockets. We could do all that and still get back ahead of our fellow prisoners who were still on the march.

We bade a hasty goodbye to the German family after a hearty breakfast of farm eggs and bacon, and flagged down the first fast-looking van that came down the road heading east. 'Hop in, chaps,' came the invitation when we begged a lift. With an unbelievable stroke of luck we had unwittingly picked the mobile command post of the brigade commander who had been to a divisional conference and was now on his way to the front again to catch up with his troops. The brigadier was quite young and very friendly. As we sped past trucks and tanks, with the driver heading east to the front of the tank column, he explained to us at his map table how the battle was going and queried us about how we found conditions on the German side of the line.

'What camp were you chaps in?' queried the brigadier.

We explained the many camps we had experienced, much to his surprise.

'How did they treat you?' he asked.

'Not bad,' I replied. 'They broadly followed the Geneva Convention for the treatment of prisoners and treated us fairly, for the most part.'

'Just as well,' he said. 'We're catching up with them rapidly and they're about to answer for all their ill-treatment of prisoners, particularly the Russians.'

He dropped us off at a freshly occupied village and I asked the first civilian I saw where I could find the mayor.

I located his house and knocked on his door. It opened slowly to reveal a thin, rather nervous man who was obviously scared.

'Haben sie ein auto?' (Do you have a car?) I demanded in as threatening a voice as I could muster. He answered in the affirmative.

'Wir mussen es requirieren fur militarische zweck.' (We need to commandeer it for military purposes.)

'Becommen sie es bitte.' (Get it please.)

It did not take us long to discover that he had an Opel in good condition and with our new luxurious mode of transport we proceeded to move happily out of the village as soon as we could.

We were on our way when we took our first and last prisoner as we were heading for the nearest petrol dump. A fully armed German soldier — a mere lad it seemed to us — appeared from the bushes at the roadside and indicated that he wanted to surrender. We were glad about that because the road was quiet at that point and we were unarmed. I spoke to him in German and accepted his surrender and then relieved him of his rifle while Herb took his bayonet. I cocked his gun and we marched him off to custody in a British Army unit further down the road. Before we handed him over I took possession of his steel helmet and ripped his shoulder badges off as souvenirs. I have them to this day.

The drive to Brussels was not easy. At all times we were going against the traffic and were continually directed by military police to pull over and wait for the lengthy convoys to pass. At another point we had to take a lengthy and time-consuming detour to avoid an SS division which was still holding out in a forest area adjacent to the main route where heavy fighting was still continuing. The SS did not take prisoners. We stopped occasionally to scrounge food from the mobile cookhouses along the route.

We finally arrived, exhausted, at Brussels. There we were compelled to seek succour in hospital because we had both become quite ill. It was only doggedness and the knowledge that Brussels was one step from Paris that kept us going for the last few hours. Nausea and diarrhoea had taken a hold of us, no doubt induced in part by reaction to the rich foods we were now consuming. We were kept under treatment and observation in the American military hospital for three days. I must say that although we were anxious to get on our way we appreciated the short stay as we were racked with nausea, dog-tired and needed the rest.

That three-day break gave us time to rest and think. The result was a drastic change of plans.

'Alex,' said Herb, 'after these last three days I'm wondering how we're going to find it in Paris. I s'pose there'll be more chaos there than there is here with all the Froggies flocking to their beloved Paris. I'm beginning to have doubts about the wisdom of trying to get there. I haven't recovered from the spell in hospital yet.'

'Yeah,' I agreed. 'But what about the money we'll get for the car? I would hate to forfeit that.'

'Let's see if we can get a seat on a plane going to England,' Herb suggested. 'And if we can then maybe we can sell the car here.'

I concurred and we put our plan into action.

We decided to get to England as fast as we could. Aircraft were flying back from Brussels almost non-stop but it was impossible to get on one of them. The waiting time in the queue for ex-prisoners was weeks!

Chapter 29

Impossible? Not quite. There are always ways and means for inventive minds. We located the RAF area transport officer who was a young flight lieutenant responsible for allocating seats on the aircraft heading back to England so we engaged him in serious discussion. It appeared that he did not have transport of his own and was thus hampered in his movements. We on the other hand had a nice vehicle but we could not drive it to England. We seemed to have the basic elements needed for a mutually advantageous and simple solution to our problems. Less than an hour later we were aboard a Lancaster headed for England and the transport officer was the proud owner of a nice Opel. We handed over the keys to the car as we boarded the aircraft. By that time we were so homesick that in our book it was a good swap!

CHAPTER 30
HOME SWEET HOME, 1945

As the rich green fields of England sped beneath the wings of our aircraft we really did start to feel convinced that we were once more in the world of the living. With my first step onto the Lancaster I had quit the Belgian earth and severed physical contact with a group of countries which had spelled hardship and danger, hunger and misery for almost four years. Freedom and a normal social life beckoned!

The fields of England were so green as our aircraft flew in over the Wash that they tugged at our heart strings. The import of what had happened in the last week was now sinking in. We were overwhelmed by the realisation that we could now do what we liked, within reason. Everything looked wonderful. Upon landing we were escorted to a large medical building by our friendly WAAFs, enough to raise our blood pressure beyond normal, but once inside we were brought down to reality as we were stripped of all our clothes and deloused. Then came some new clothes and a thorough medical examination followed by a debriefing by RAF Intelligence.

To my open-mouthed surprise the RAF Intelligence officer who interrogated me was no other than Alfie, now Flight Lieutenant AFP James of MI5.

'As you know,' he said, 'I was repatriated because of the burns to my face which affected my sight permanently and prevented me from flying again. Actually it didn't, but my spin was sufficient to con the Germans into sending me home. I then simply rejoined MI5. All the other stuff I pedalled in the stalag was a bit of bullshit, which I think you guessed. It's good fun to see how much the gullible public will take from a good story-teller. Although I must say I think some of

186

mine were really too outrageous. Look me up when you get out of the clutches of the WAAFs. In a fortnight's time I'll be in Oxford, reading in international affairs. You'll find me in Balliol.'

Upon mature reflection, subsequently, I supposed it wasn't so strange as I had always thought that Alfie was in some way connected with Intelligence. Even so, it was a coincidence that we met like that. We had a good chin-wag before I was then sent to hospital in Brighton.

Brighton was where the headquarters of the RAAF was established and Herbie and I saw increasing numbers of RAAF aircrew streaming in as the war drew to a close. We were enjoying a wonderful convalescence in the Brighton hospital and saw no reason to tell the attractive and sympathetic nurses that we were feeling well enough to be discharged. We had not yet seen any of our friends from Stalag 357. They were still being held prisoner by the Germans. But we saw many new aircrew because pilots and navigators and gunners had now become redundant and were waiting to be allotted to a boat heading home. Many of them were frustrated as they had not had a chance to fly on operations.

We heard that just down the road, at Eastbourne, were the Australian Army ex-prisoners. That was where the Australian Army had established their headquarters. I took a bus there one day hoping to run into some friends from the West Australian battalions that were mauled in the Middle East, particularly in Greece and Tobruk and El Alamein. Many from my old battalion — the 16th — had been taken prisoner.

I saw this Australian officer coming down the street on the opposite side to me and it was not long before he got close enough to recognise. 'Hey, Lex!' I cried. 'Where are you going?'

He stopped, took a good look at me and exclaimed, 'Alex Kerr! What a pleasant surprise. I was going down to Brighton to see if I knew any friends in the air force. I knew you had become a pilot but I didn't expect to run into you here.'

'Well,' I said, 'I was on my way to the Aussie camp because I was sure I would know some of the boys from the second eleventh and the second sixteenth who were taken prisoner in the Middle East. I didn't specifically expect to see you but since I have I can give you something I have been saving for this encounter.' With that I produced from my tunic a letter addressed to Lex. When he looked at it he was speechless for a moment. Then I explained how I had come by it.

I had picked it up purely by chance when on an impulse I bent down to examine spilt mail from a bombed-out train during my escape in Germany. I was so surprised to see a letter addressed to someone I knew that I kept it to give to Lex in the hope that he had survived the war. He dined out on that story for many years after the war.

I decided that while in Britain I should see as much of the country as possible at government expense as I might not get the chance to return for some years. Consequently, as soon as I was able after my discharge from hospital, I travelled to Scotland to stay with my maiden aunts on the Isle of Arran, in the Firth of Clyde, and to see Glasgow and Edinburgh and other Scottish attractions before returning to London. It was great to relax and take walks in the highlands.

From there I made my way back to RAAF headquarters in Brighton and took the chance to enrol in a course for service men and women at Balliol College, Oxford University. That was a three-week course and I found it very interesting to live in as a student in Balliol. We dined at table every night with the Master of Balliol, Lord Lindsay, presiding. There it was that I met Alfie James once more. He was reading in international affairs and standing as a member of the newly formed Commonwealth Party in the forthcoming general elections. (Further encounters took place in Perth after the war and subsequently Alfie, who had joined the Church of England as editor of its journal, made world headlines when he was imprisoned in China in the early 1970s. He was charged with espionage and finally released only after protracted negotiations between the Australian and Chinese governments during which Prime Minister Whitlam flew to China to intercede on his behalf. I met up with him later in Sydney and Perth and we lunched at each other's club in 1991. He is the most remarkable person I have ever met.)

After Balliol I visited Stratford on Avon and then went down to Devon to stay with my observer, Bill Legg. After his repatriation Bill had remained in the RAF. He had been commissioned and was based near his home in Dorset. Bill was able to get around but the wound in his back had never healed. It remained open until he died many years later. We chewed the rag for a few days until I thought I should report back to base.

Back in London, I visited London University to see whether my exam papers had arrived from Germany. As might be expected, they hadn't. But to my surprise I discovered that the intermediate B.Sc exams were being held that week. Although I had not done any study for about nine months, I asked to be allowed to sit them again and was granted permission. So off I went with a bar of chocolate. Eyebrows were raised as I munched on chocolate while writing my papers. I didn't explain that this was routine in prison camp.

(Some months later, when I was a student at the University of Western Australia, I was informed that I had passed those exams and a year after that I was informed, to my surprise, that my exam papers from Germany had finally arrived and I had passed them too.)

Then along came what we had all been waiting for — Victory in Europe Day. The war in Europe was over. Britons heaved a collective sigh of relief and thanks and began to express the emotions that they had been bottling up over several years. Throughout Britain crowds mushroomed in the cities as people cheered and danced in the streets. The main street in Brighton was a mixture of the RAAF blue and the colourful dresses of office girls and the white uniforms of the nurses and the uniforms of the navy and army. We danced, it seems, for hours. The outpouring of emotion was overwhelming. No more killing or maiming. Promises to return could be kept. No longer would the dreaded telegrams arrive to announce the bad news. The war in the Pacific was temporarily forgotten, though there were destined to be many more casualties before the Japanese surrendered some three months later.

I felt a great sense of relief. The war that so quickly followed the war to end all wars was finally over — at least the major part of it, centred on Europe and the Middle East. There was still another segment to come in Asia and the Pacific, but it seemed to be coming closer at an increasing rate. I was reminded of the feelings I had when Herb and I became free men again. We could breathe easier and no longer had to keep looking over our shoulder. There was no longer violence hanging over Europe's head, no longer loss of both military and civilian lives, no longer deadly bombing. People could start to breathe easier and dared to dream of a life free of the spectre of war.

In fact it was when I was in the mid-Pacific on the *Iberia*, coming home in September, that the glad news came through. Hirohito had capitulated after the Hiroshima and Nagasaki bombs had been dropped. We were on an armed vessel and the captain gave orders for the boat to fire all its weapons in salvos to mark the end of hostilities. For a deafening half-hour the air was filled with the acrid smell of cordite and our ears were assailed with the roar of the guns while the crew and passengers cheered as the boat ploughed its way towards Sydney.

The non-commissioned aircrew had all been promoted during their imprisonment to warrant officer and, all spruced up with our new uniforms, we arrived at the dock in Fremantle to a large crowd of parents and friends, there to greet their sons and friends who had survived. While we were overjoyed to be home we were only too conscious of the many we would never see again, friends whose lives were cut off when they were just really beginning. It was a very emotional time.

But these thoughts faded temporarily as we embraced our families and immersed ourselves in the joyous reunions.

From the colourful, crowded Fremantle wharf teeming with blue uniforms and bright dresses we made our way to our car and home. I looked around with delight and recognition as we finally drove down Northwood Street. I pondered on my unbelievable good luck over the last four years and wondered how many of the neighbourhood kids I would see in the next week or two. I knew that my best friend, Bob Blair, who lived around the corner, lost his life over Holland flying Halifaxes, and Ian Ingle, who lived next door, lost his life in Darwin flying Kittyhawks. How many more?

We pulled into the drive and my family disappeared, leaving me alone at the front door. This was pre-arranged by me in a recent letter in which I said that I wished to be left to knock on the front door and greet my family as if returning from a holiday. I knocked, my mother opened the door and we all embraced. And that was my homecoming — delight tinged with sadness.

Chapter 30

Walking through the streets of Perth, visiting WA Newspapers, where I worked before the war, riding out to the beaches I used to frequent, was all part of returning to normality. It was not long before I was able to fly to Melbourne to see my cousin Pat, who had treated us so well when we were trainees and who had written to me and contributed to my welcome mail in prison. There I met John Thomas, Pat's fiancé, who was a dentist in the RAAF. I remember getting sunburnt in Melbourne in October — something I had previously believed to be impossible!

When I returned from Melbourne I discovered that I was supposed to undergo some therapy to assist in my recovery from the traumatic experience I had had as a prisoner. As I did not consider it traumatic but rather exciting and overall beneficial, I was somewhat bemused. Nevertheless I enjoyed the rehabilitation treatment we received at Yanchep, particularly the great meals and the daily ration of beer.

Thinking of traumatic experiences led me to contemplate prison life and its effect on me. On my return I found that all my family and friends considered that my time in prison must have been a waste of four miserable years and sympathised with me. On the contrary I felt that I had been lucky in many ways to have had the experience and to have lived through it.

I had grown in self-confidence and assumed leadership roles in many activities in the camp. I had played many different sports and read countless books — not many novels but mainly documentaries — all of which expanded my general knowledge. I had taken a positive view of life and had been determined to take every opportunity while in camp to improve my lot in life.

I gradually realised that being shot down was the best thing that could have happened to me, given the casualty rate in Bomber Command. Had I remained flying I would, without much doubt, have been killed. Out of the 126,000 aircrew in Bomber Command, there were 76,000 casualties. Of the original 40 members of my No. 1 course only 12 remained alive at the end of the war and nine of those were POWs.

It was clear in retrospect that a bomber pilot's best chance of living was to get shot down and survive! Those who volunteered early had the greatest chance of being killed simply through the efflux of time.

For these reasons I felt that, given the timing, nature and extent of my injuries, I had been given a reprieve and that I was henceforth living on borrowed time so I should live every day to the fullest.

As might be expected those few homecoming months were a time of parties and reunions as soldiers, sailors and airmen drifted home from their various theatres of war to reunions with their families and friends. But slowly the euphoria ebbed until the returned service personnel girded their loins and faced up to the task of finding a job and carving out a career for themselves, taking with them memories of a conflict which had changed their lives forever.

EPILOGUE

Chapters 1 to 6 were drafted after the war as an introduction to the written record that I kept of my time as a prisoner in Germany.

The chapters that followed were, for the most part, a verbatim copy of a secret diary I kept while a POW. (I have added dialogue here and there.) I wanted to keep a record of life in a prison camp. This part of my life constituted a very important and fundamental episode which left an indelible imprint on me. The original diary still exists as a faded exercise book with minute handwriting in pencil. It accompanied me throughout my incarceration, sometimes stuffed under my shirt, sometimes hidden in my bedding but always eluding the German searchers. Here and there I have made minor corrections to the original script when subsequent information has shown the original to be incorrect. The transcribing of the original handwritten script to a computerised story has taken me quite some time but in the doing it has proved to be a most rewarding exercise. Why? Because it has brought back to me the vivid memories of a unique part of my life.

Chapter 30 was written after the conflict was over in order to tidy up the loose ends left in my story after Herbie and I had gained our freedom. I felt that it was of importance to conserve the original on-the-spot record of a part of the military history of World War II.

Over those 70-odd years since the adventure started, some links have stayed stronger than others. For many years I kept in touch with members of my crew, particularly my navigator, Bill Legg, who was never free of his war wounds and finally succumbed in the 1990s. I am still enjoying my occasional links in person or by phone with my rear gunner, Dave Fraser, who remains healthy in his 90's and still attends POW reunions.

Cal Younger, an Australian pilot, settled in England after the war but we kept our friendship going with occasional visits both ways until he died in 2014. He was a cartoonist and a writer and we had a lot in common. Cal wrote the popular *No Flight from the Cage* describing life in a POW camp. He played an active role in the administration of the RAF Ex-POW Association for many years.

In 1990, through an amazing coincidence, I met, via correspondence, the German pilot who shot me down, Eckart-Wilhelm von Bonin. There were many mysteries and unanswered questions that night and he solved some of them for me. It was his first downing. He went on to become an ace with 41 victories. We maintained a steady correspondence for a short time thereafter. He died in 1992.

I enclose a verbatim extract from von Bonin's first letter to me in June 1990. In this and subsequent letters from him I was able to ascertain some answers to questions that had puzzled me for half a century.

Dear Professor Kerr,

Many thanks for your kind letter. It is a good feeling to get so friendly lines from a former adversary and I am very grateful to Steve Martin that he succeeded in finding out your address. It was extremely interesting for me to learn how it was truly in fact in those days.

When we visited the Wellington at that time in Tonning we could see only few entry holes. Therefore I was also every time of the opinion that all men had survived. Now, I am sorry to read, that one of your comrades met his death, and, when in those days I was a bit ashamed that I had forgotten the button for the 2cm guns, so I am glad about, then, when I had hit with the 2cm it would have been far more bad for you all.

In the course of my activities as a night fighter I never aimed at the rear gunner but only at the wings with the containers. By that the aircraft should have burned, but so that the crew could parachute even then. Mostly I succeeded in this way but many times the aircraft burst. Later on, you know, there were only four engines aircrafts we had to do with.

Altogether I had 41 successes and got the Knight Cross of the Iron Cross early in 1944. Since autumn 1943 I was a group commander and since summer 1944 a major. ...

... Once more many thanks for your kind letter. With my best greetings I remain yours sincerely, von Bonin.

I am deeply indebted to Steve Martin from Toronto, Canada, who was an avid collector of Luftwaffe memorabilia after the war. By chance in the 1980s he came across some photos of a burnt-out Wellington and after several years of research he discovered the names and addresses of both the Wellington crew (it was our aircraft) and the German pilot who shot us down. He then put us in touch with each other. This fascinating story with all its coincidental twists and turns was due to the persistence and dedication of Steve Martin.

When I cast my memory back, I find that I think mostly of that four-year period, especially in England when I was on operational flying training and then on operations. The flying part was dangerous, adrenaline-pumping and exciting, and the non-flying part was dancing, drinking, listening to Vera Lynn, and enjoying life to the full. Everyone was aware of what the following day might bring. It was like one big unreal continuous party, lasting for years. Fun and danger alternating like night and day — so exciting.

My colleagues were almost all within the narrow age group of 19 to 25 years. Before we were shot down we lived just for the day. Death was not discussed though it occurred every night. Back from missions, aircrew were mostly more interested in bacon and eggs than in conditions over the target. The uniforms seemed to add an air of gaiety to everything. Few of the young aircrew ever thought of tomorrow.

When tomorrow came for some of us, POW camp curtailed our activities and imposed a somewhat boring routine upon us all, broken now and again by episodes of danger. Gone were the parties and dances. In an environment characterised by extremes of hunger, fatigue, cold and misery, one became experienced in recognising in one's fellow prisoners such aspects of character as trustworthiness, ability to withstand stress and setbacks, leadership, calmness in crisis. Friends made in circumstances like these remained friends for life.

The most stimulating and uplifting and exciting of my times in POW camp were the three occasions when I was not in POW camp, that is, when I was on the loose after escaping. There was a feeling of triumph and excitement when we were on the run and had to depend on our wits to maintain our freedom and maybe our lives. It was an exhilarating feeling knowing you were winning a dangerous cat and mouse game with maybe a disastrous result if you lost. The adrenaline was coursing through your veins almost continuously.

In reading accounts of ex-prisoners in many different circumstances, and talking to them during and after their ordeal, I come across references to the fact that they think of their POW experiences as something that was either a rewarding and worthwhile experience, or the most horrible and degrading existence they had been forced to endure. I think the latter would particularly be so with the prisoners of the Japanese. I personally never thought of my own experience as horrible and degrading.

But I do recognise these sentiments as very real. Speaking for myself, I always, during that period, saw the beneficial aspects of life as more important to me than the negative aspects. I have to thank my parents for giving me a gene that stimulated me to learn, to enquire, to dig around for facts and opinions and to keep on trying to expand my knowledge. It stood me in good stead when I was a prisoner and made me stronger, wiser and more tolerant. I read hundreds of books and made notes of all that I read. It also fitted me so well for a return to life in Civvy Street.

Because I was inherently optimistic I was fortunate. I was able, much more than some of my fellow prisoners, to bear the vicissitudes of incarceration with fortitude because they did not seem so important to me at the time. As a consequence, I weathered the storm well. I came out of prison thankful that my life had so miraculously been saved. I determined that I would make the most of the reprieve I had been given. I would live every day to the fullest. Friends back home were astounded when I said — and meant it — that being taken prisoner was the best thing that could have happened to me. I wasn't thinking of aircrew survival statistics when I said that but when I saw those statistics some years later it only reinforced my opinion. That was 70 years ago — how lucky was I? What did this horrific conflict achieve?

Without a doubt the Battle of Britain saved Britain from invasion in 1940. Without a doubt, the intensity of the Bomber Command night offensive, in 1943–4, supported by the USAAF day offensive crippled the German war machine and destroyed her industrial power. Without a doubt Generals Patton and Montgomery in the Middle East and Europe displayed the armoured strength in 1944 which rapidly pushed the German forces back to their homeland. Earlier, the US naval forces under Admiral Nimitz had dealt a devastating blow to Japan in the Battle of Midway, which turned the tide in the Pacific War and saved Australia from invasion. Later Marshal Timoschenko, the commander of the Russian Army, overran the mighty German Army at Stalingrad and kept on going to Berlin.

So, in terms of lost ground regained and of new states with new governments created and of new and threatening power alignments, a great deal happened to the political map of the world in that relatively short period. But a great deal also happened to the demographic map of the world, much to the sorrow and distress of many countries; most of it due, at least in the early years, to the grotesque, twisted mind of one Austrian madman, assisted by the even greater evil of Stalin.

It is estimated that the cost of World War II, in terms of human life, was 30 million souls. At one stage the Germans held 11 million prisoners and the Japanese held unknown millions. If one adds the stress and misery felt by those prisoners over the five or six years of conflict to the sorrow and misery felt by the civilians whose families and homes were destroyed by bombing, the immense cost of the war is overwhelming.

It was probably the stark realisation that such a holocaust could happen again in a flash that finally brought the leaders of the United States and Russia to their senses and to the conviction that the Cold War should end. Since Perestroika, 25 years have elapsed. Let us hope that the twisted minds of some of the current day national leaders are not allowed to run riot and once more cause mayhem. And let us hope that the leaders of the major nations will never again lead us to the brink.

ACKNOWLEDGEMENTS

I have many people to thank for assistance with this book. It originally began life as a war diary. When family and friends encouraged me to expand it to include the early family history it grew considerably in size and scope.

I have, first, to thank my brother, Langford, and sister, Freda, who are now deceased. They were much older than me and were thus able to recall early times in the family before I was born. My son, Ian, during a visit we made to the Isle of Arran in Scotland, researched the early history of the Kerrs of Lochranza and provided a link with the remote past.

The war diary section owes much to the friends I made in the war years. My great friend Sel (or Nobby) Clark, after sharing with me the year-long build-up to operational flying duties, made a date in London which he kept but I didn't. We resumed our friendship after the war. My navigator, Bill Legg, and my rear gunner, Dave Fraser, shared my days in Germany and our friendship carried on for years afterwards.

Thousands of aircrew prisoners of war shared their incarceration with me and constituted the environmental background of my life for nigh on four years. Some of them stood out. Cal Younger made his mark in a different way, as author and cartoonist, and remained a good friend until his death in London in 2014. Herb Crump, with whom I eventually escaped, remained a close friend but died in Adelaide at an early age. Canadians Ivan Quinn and Don Sugden together with Jock Alexander, with whom I shared the administrative office in No. 39 Hut, remained firm friends after the war and as a group we met up many times at POW reunions in England and Canada. These all made a positive contribution to this tale and I thank them for their friendship.

When it came to putting my writings into book form, I have first to thank my wife, Joan, and in more recent years my children Ian, Penny, Robyn, Andy and Rosie for their love, encouragement, comments and support as the book progressed. Robyn and Rosie particularly spent many hours on formatting, editing and illustration. I can't thank them enough for the time they put in and the quality of their advice. My thanks also go to Jenny Scepanovic for the assistance she gave me in the editing of the manuscript and to Denny Neave of Big Sky Publishing for his advice and support with publishing matters.

Many friends from the Military History Association and Air Force Association provided useful comments, in particular authors Bill Edgar and Russell Mehan. Chris Allen, another author, was most helpful in pointing me towards Big Sky Publishing. To all these, and other friends, I owe my heartfelt thanks.

Alex Kerr